Inge and Sten Hegeler, both doctors and psychologists of professional standing, have followed their bestselling book, *The XYZ of Love*, with this sympathetic and very readable work in which they sum up what, in the opinion of the authors, is the surest way of achieving a happy and satisfying sex life.

Also by Inge and Sten Hegeler

The XYZ of Love

Inge and Sten Hegeler

Living is Loving

Translated from the Danish by David Hohnen

Drawings by Eiler Krag

A PANTHER BOOK

GRANADA
London Toronto Sydney New York

Published by Granada Publishing Limited in 1974
Reprinted 1979, 1981

ISBN 0 586 04070 6

First published in Great Britain by
Neville Spearman Ltd 1971
Copyright © Inge and Sten Hegeler
Fredenksbergallé 25, DK-1820 V, Denmark 1971

Granada Publishing Limited
Frogmore, St Albans, Herts AL2 2NF
and
3 Upper James Street, London W1R 4BP
866 United Nations Plaza, New York, NY 10017, USA
117 York Street, Sydney, NSW 2000, Australia
100 Skyway Avenue, Rexdale, Ontario, M9W 3A6, Canada
PO Box 84165, Greenside, 2034, Johannesburg, South Africa
61 Beach Road, Auckland, New Zealand

Made and printed in Great Britain by
Hazell Watson & Viney Ltd,
Aylesbury, Bucks
Set in Linotype Times

Contents

A sexual relationship completely devoid of problems isn't the key to happiness. It would soon become trivial and boring.

i&sh

What do a man and a woman experience during sexual intercourse?

We so often hear people say that all this sexual enlightenment is unnecessary. 'What did they do in the Stone Age?' they ask with a grin and add, 'After all, it's something any reasonably intelligent poodle can manage.'

Well, both human beings and animals are certainly capable of reproducing their own kind without any form of instruction. But perhaps we could point out that one of the differences between human beings and animals is precisely the fact that we human beings have developed sexual relationships from being a purely animal mating act to something that is close to being an art – at any rate for some people.

In order to breed children it is only necessary for the man to reach a climax, in other words have an orgasm. From the point of view of propagating the human species the woman's orgasm is utterly immaterial. Cynical men can therefore claim that provided *they* enjoy themselves everything in the garden is lovely.

And that is really how things were once upon a time. In our grandparents' days any lady worthy of the name could go to her doctor and ask for a sedative if she felt anything faintly like a sexual urge welling up inside her.

So today perhaps some people will think it's a little extravagant of us to claim that a woman should be allowed to derive some pleasure from sexual intercourse too, and that this is only reasonable.

But you probably have to be a very rabid anti-feminist to maintain that sort of viewpoint for long.

'Are you really trying to claim that a marriage can't be happy unless the woman has an orgasm during sexual intercourse with her husband?'

We've heard that question so often.

The answer is that a woman *can* be happy in her marriage without getting anything out of it sexually.

But an extremely large number of women find it a very great strain on the relationship if they have no opportunity of getting any pleasure out of their sex lives.

Recent research has proved that any form of sex play produces an accumulation of tensions of various kinds in a woman (certain tissues become filled with blood, for instance) even if she doesn't actually feel very much and even if she remains far from having an orgasm the whole time. This results in a feeling of dissatisfaction and restlessness during the next few hours and can be unpleasant for her.

THERE IS NO SUCH THING AS A FRIGID WOMAN!

One would think that women without sexual feelings, completely cold women, so-called 'frigid women', would be able to enjoy a happy marriage without sex.

Unfortunately quite a number of men would be prepared to swear that their wives are cold, absolutely uninterested in sex, in other words frigid. Thank heavens they are wrong!

There is no such thing as a frigid woman. Women who are completely devoid of the ability to react sexually, in other words have no interest in sex whatsoever, simply do not exist.

But of course there are women who are very interested in sex, and women who are not so interested in sex.

However, the difference between the two types is not as great as their husbands perhaps think.

8

A knowledgeable, patient, but at the same time persistent and imaginative man can get an apparently frigid and uninterested woman very close to becoming a 'very interested' type.

Wardell B. Pomery, one of Kinsey's closest associates, relates that he and Kinsey had the opportunity of observing a 60-year-old woman, who had an orgasm within 2 to 5 seconds after sexual intercourse had commenced!

This 60-year-old woman did not only react exceptionally fast but was also capable of having between 15 and 50 orgasms within 20 minutes.

Hearing about a sexual athlete like this may give many women an inferiority complex, but it should be borne in mind that she is one of the most remarkable cases known to science. One can safely call her abnormally quick to react sexually.

In fact, the reason why we mention her at all is because there is something else about her we would like to emphasize: She was apparently frigid until she reached her fortieth year!

Throughout her entire life prior to this time she had never had an orgasm during sexual intercourse or any form of sex play with a man.

HOW IMPORTANT IS SEX TO A MARRIAGE?

In 1953, an American named C. R. Adams published an investigation into the degree of marital bliss enjoyed by a hundred and fifty married women seen in relation to the sexual enjoyment they derived from marriage.

Adams proved that the greater the amount of sexual enjoyment a woman claimed to derive from her marriage, the happier she believed herself to be.

Adams did not try to say that this was a rule to which there were no exceptions. If all other aspects of her marriage are satisfactory a woman is perfectly capable of feeling happy – even if her sex life does not exactly function as it might do. Furthermore, he also encountered

9

women who thought they were unhappy in their marriages despite the fact that the sexual side of their relationship functioned perfectly well.

But when he divided the one hundred and fifty women into three groups according to their ability to react sexually he found an overwhelming majority of women with happy marriages in the group which reacted best sexually. Other investigations point in the same direction. One hundred and eighty-one women who declared that their marriages were happy were compared with a group of two hundred and ten women who were divorced. It appeared that 90% of the happily married women were positively interested. They stated that sexual relationships gave them pleasure while only 53% of the divorced women had got on well sexually in their marriages. And from marriage consultants we know that 3 out of 4 persons who seek their help have sexual problems.

It is not only of importance to a man and his wife that

Children sometimes find it difficult to understand that they were begotten in a moment of love

their marriage is a happy one – it naturally has an effect on the children, too. Many of us have experienced parents who quarrelled, fought, or who were quite simply unfriendly to each other.

Can we not agree that this is a poor background for children who themselves may marry in due course and try to live with another person?

And if this is the case, namely that sexual pleasure plays a not unimportant role in a good marriage, it must also be of importance for them to see whether their parents are capable of having a lovely time together.

THREE GOLDEN RULES

What qualifications are required of two people who want to reach the state of being able to have a lovely time together?

For it doesn't seem to be the kind of state anybody at all is capable of reaching unaided – as so many people believe.

1. First, you must be able to talk to each other about these things.

It sounds so banal, but time and again when two people start explaining their marital problems it turns out that they are incapable of discussing the things which really affect them and their lives together.

What makes it so difficult?

It's probably got something to do with the fact that so few people are capable of accepting themselves. They are dissatisfied with themselves and think that everybody else is better and has an easier time of it. And if you can't accept yourself you can't accept the other person's admiration and love either. He must be a fool to love me, I'm such a failure and so hopeless!

2. You should be able to accept yourself the way you are.

If you can't do this you can't accept your partner either.

Another question: How do you get as far as being able to approve of yourself? How do you set about liking yourself?

3. You should know something about how other people feel. In other words, you should know what is normal.

We know that others eat when they are hungry. We know they hold their knife and fork more or less the same way as we do. We know that it is difficult for most people to eat spaghetti tidily and that most people like rissoles and pancakes.

But when it's a question of people's sex lives and how they live together we don't know so very much about the

A wall of this kind is to be found in all too many homes

Smiths and Joneses and their problems and their favourite dishes.

We hear quite a lot, we read quite a lot, and much of what we hear is superstition, exaggeration, boasting and misunderstanding. All of which helps to give us a sense of failure and the feeling that other people just don't have any problems at all. But it's not true.

THE BOUNDS OF WHAT IS 'NORMAL' ARE VERY WIDE

If we didn't see other people and their height were kept a secret we might, for example, form the idea that all other men were six feet tall and all other women five feet six inches – and that it was only we ourselves who were so incredibly tall or so ridiculously short.

But it so happens that we know that most men are between five feet six inches and five feet ten inches, and that it is not at all unusual for a man to be taller or shorter than this. We know that it is not until a man is six feet eight inches or more that we can talk about anything unusual, something abnormal. We know that women as a rule are between five feet and five feet six inches and that very few grown women are shorter than four feet ten inches.

In other words, we know what is normal and usual and by no means very exceptional – when it comes to our height.

But when it comes to sex, or sexual relationships, or whatever one likes to call it, many people seem to be lonely and unhappy. They feel themselves to be abnormal, frigid, or perverse – according to whatever dreadful label other people have pasted on them – but as a rule entirely without justification!

There are many definitions of happiness. None of them is completely satisfactory, but generally there is a grain of truth in all of them – perhaps in ours too:

13

Happiness is knowing what is normal – and 'normal' covers a wide range.

In this book we shall give an account of the latest observations made in the sphere of sexual relationships between human beings. Perhaps in this way we shall help some of our readers to obtain greater knowledge as to what is usual and normal, and thus enable them to begin to accept themselves and their partners. Later, perhaps they will be able to talk to each other about matters which really do concern the most intimate aspects of their relationship.

It was Professor Alfred Kinsey who with his Kinsey Report opened a door which hitherto had been closed: the door to our knowledge of other people's sexual relationships. Kinsey was obliged to ask people how they got on: 'What do you do?'

Masters and Johnson * are two other Americans who, thanks to Kinsey's pioneer work, had the courage to go a step further. They were permitted to observe people both masturbating and making love, and in this way were given an opportunity of checking not only what we say we do but also whether we describe matters correctly. What do you *really* do?

* William Masters is a gynaecologist. Virginia Johnson is a psychologist. Together they have observed more than 10,000 orgasms. More than 10,000 times they have watched a woman, or a man, or a couple reach a sexual climax. Their study material consisted of approximately 700 people of whom a couple of hundred or so were married couples. Sometimes the persons under observation reached the point of orgasm through masturbation and some couples would enable each other to have orgasms by means of sexual stimulation of one kind or another.

The observations made by these two Americans were collected in a report entitled *Human Sexual Response,* published in the USA in 1966.

There is nothing the slightest bit pornographic about the book. It is a relatively dry, not exactly easily-read account of the results obtained by the two researchers. The same applies to the authors' latest book *Sexual Inadequacy.*

Large parts of this material can be found in somewhat more digestible form in R. and E. Brecher's book *An Analysis of Human Sexual Response.*

OUR NEEDS HAVE THREE PHASES

Common to all human needs is the fact that they can be divided into several phases. We need to drink, to sleep, to eat, and to do many other things. And, as a rule, each need can be divided into three phases.

1. The need, or desire, is aroused, and our interest begins to increase.

For example, we feel thirsty. The feeling begins to recur with increasing frequency. Finally, we can hardly think of anything else.

Or, we feel sleepy, we begin to yawn, and finally we can hardly keep our eyes open.

We happen to think of food – our mouths begin to water – after a while we feel really hungry, and finally we are overwhelmed by hunger.

2. The need is satisfied.

We drink, we sleep, or we eat.

It feels wonderful. We enjoy a cool glass of beer as it runs down our throat. We enjoy lying down and closing our eyes, or we eat our dinner with great relish.

3. The need has disappeared for a while. We are not interested.

We have no thought of drinking or sleeping – and feel no interest in exciting dishes.

MASTERS AND JOHNSON FOUND
FOUR PHASES

Masters and Johnson worked with the same three phases when conducting their investigations into the sexual need, but they found it practical to introduce a kind of extra phase which they called *the plateau phase*.

They did so because in both sexes special things begin to happen towards the end of the first phase when the need is mounting.

The plateau phase in both the woman and the man is

the period immediately before the climax, or orgasm, is reached – i.e. before the sexual need is satisfied.

THE FIRST PHASE: THE PHASE OF SEXUAL EXCITEMENT

We could put things this way: First the sexual need makes itself felt, and then it becomes stimulated to a greater degree of excitement.

The outward sign of sexual excitement in the man is, of course, that the penis becomes larger and stiffer as a result of being filled with blood.

This is also known as an erection – and the penis can become erect in a few seconds. The penis becomes considerably larger when it is filled with blood. Masters and Johnson observed that a penis which is small in its relaxed state becomes very much larger when erected, whereas a large penis only becomes slightly larger. In other words, the final result is more or less the same.

In the woman, several more things take place: the vagina becomes lubricated by a secretion that is more or less exuded through the vaginal walls. Many men believe that this is a sign that the woman is now very excited, but they are wrong. The fact that the vagina becomes moist is a sign that the woman is beginning to get excited, in other words, that she is beginning to react sexually.

Thus a woman is by no means ready for coition just because her vagina has gone moist – which can happen in less than 30 seconds.

Just above the opening to the vagina is a little sort of button known as the clitoris. Just like a man's penis, it is a very sensitive organ as it is provided with a great many nerves. Just like the penis, the clitoris is a kind of rod that ends in a little knob. This knob is particularly sensitive. Just like the penis, the clitoris, during this phase, becomes filled with blood and therefore stiffer and more protruding. It actually corresponds, anatomically speaking, to the knob, or *glans* of the man's penis. So it is only logical that

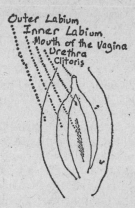

Schematic drawing of the female sexual organ

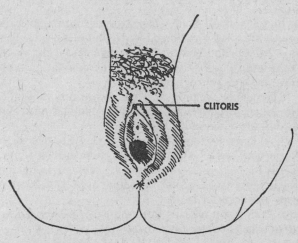

*The drawing shows what a woman looks like from underneath
when she's got her legs bent*

it should be the centre of a woman's lustful feelings.

The clitoris is a woman's most sensitive point.

Many men believe that the vagina is the place where a woman experiences her most intense feelings of sexual lust. But they are wrong. And this, in particular, is probably the misunderstanding which has prevented many women from deriving enjoyment from sexual intercourse. But we shall return to this in a later chapter.

It is true that the clitoris is indirectly stimulated by virtue of the fact that the movements of the penis inside the vagina are more or less transplanted through the smaller vaginal lips at the entrance to the vagina. However, it is still only an indirect form of stimulation which is very seldom sufficient to give a woman an orgasm.

But we must stress the fact that Masters and Johnson found that no matter whether the clitoris was small or large, no matter whether it was right at the entrance of the vagina or a little bit further up, it made no difference whatsoever to the woman's ability to have an orgasm.

The important thing was that the woman herself *realized* that her clitoris was the focal centre of her sexual desires.

In the woman, as her sexual excitement mounts, other organs are filled with blood too. Her nipples become larger and firmer – and thereafter the area round them becomes filled with blood so that it looks as though the nipples have become smaller again.

The smaller vaginal lips, which are normally not so prominent, become filled with blood and thus push a little against the outer, larger vaginal lips.

The inner two-thirds of the vagina become slightly longer and larger as the woman's excitement mounts towards its next phase. Most of the muscles in her body become tense, her pulse becomes faster and her blood pressure increases.

A faint blush spreads from the lower part of her body up over her stomach towards her breasts.

THE EXTRA PHASE: THE PLATEAU PHASE

As we mentioned above, Masters and Johnson discovered that when sexual excitement had reached a certain point, such important changes took place that they found it was necessary to introduce an extra phase.

In the man the plateau phase is the brief period immediately before he ejaculates. One can say that it is the period during which his ejaculation is approaching so strongly that it can no longer be stopped or delayed.

In both sexes breathing becomes quicker, the pulse beats faster, the blood pressure rises even more and the muscles become even more tense.

Some women and men increase their sexual excitement by consciously tensing their pelvic muscles.

In women what also happens is that the outermost third of the vagina becomes filled with blood and swells up. In this way the outer part of the vagina closes more tightly round the penis.

The most important thing, something we never knew before, is that the clitoris itself becomes what one might call super-sensitive and has to withdraw from the game.

Thus during the woman's plateau phase just before her orgasm, stimulation of the clitoris itself is not desirable; what is required is a more general form of stimulation of the whole region round the entrance to the vagina.

This new factor can confuse those wise and knowledgeable men who hitherto have concentrated on stimulating a woman's clitoris. Suddenly it disappears and if one tries to hunt for it, all one gets out of it is that the stimulation is interrupted, with the result that the woman doesn't have an orgasm at all.

So there is no need for either the man or the woman to let themselves become confused, but just continue with a more general stimulation of the region round the entrance to the vagina.

Late in the plateau phase the smaller vaginal lips change colour from a pale pink to a darker red. This is a sure sign that the orgasm is now approaching and that it

19

will in fact take place within $1\frac{1}{2}$ minutes providing the stimulation continues to be effective. This change of colour of the smaller vaginal lips is something Masters and Johnson have observed in all the women who took part in their investigations immediately before orgasm took place.

Thus we see that all these things that take place in the man and in the woman during the sexual excitement and plateau phases are bound up with increased tension of the muscles and swelling of blood vessels – i.e. afflux of blood.

We can also mention that during the man's plateau phase the testicles move up one at a time. We mention this because a short while ago we got a letter from an upset woman who had observed this taking place in her husband. Well, it happens to all men. In addition, Masters and Johnson described the plateau phase in the woman as the period during which her mental and physical tensions mount and mount – until her excitement is so great that she can take the hurdle over into the next phase, her actual orgasm, which is the culmination of sexual tension.

THE ORGASM ITSELF: THE CULMINATION

The woman herself knows when her orgasm is beginning because she feels a single, powerful contraction in the outer third of her vagina, almost like cramp. Then follow the clearest outer signs of the orgasm, which are relatively easy to observe: the almost rhythmical contractions in the outer part of the vagina. Curiously enough, these take place at the same intervals as the semen is squirted out through the man's penis, i.e. there is a pause lasting just under a second (0·8) between each contraction.

Masters and Johnson noted that the womb also contracts during the woman's orgasm in much the same way as during birth pains. In fact, very often – in men as well as in women – a powerful contraction of many of the muscles of the body takes place during orgasm. Many people fail to notice it at the time but the day after may be puzzled by the fact that their thighs, their back, or their pelvic muscles are aching.

Men can have good and not-so-good orgasms but the difference is less pronounced. Very few men give it much thought.

Women, on the other hand, experience to a far greater degree good and less-good orgasms. A woman can tell whether her orgasm has been intense or not.

A less powerful orgasm only gives between 3 and 5 contractions of the vaginal walls, whereas a violent, intense and powerful orgasm can give many more contractions, sometimes as many as 8 or 12.

Masters and Johnson relate that they once observed a woman have 25 contractions in 43 seconds. The intervals don't remain regular at just under a second – they become longer and longer.

A man can feel his actual orgasm beginning before there is any outward sign. Just before he ejaculates, his penis becomes even slightly larger – and then the semen is squirted out so powerfully that it can land a couple of feet away.

THE LAST PHASE: RELAXATION, SATISFACTION

In both men and women we see that orgasm results in a relief of tension, a relaxation of tensed muscles and a decrease in the swelling caused by blood in the organs concerned.

One of the first things that happens in a woman is that the region round the nipples contracts again so that it looks as if the nipples are protruding more. This happens immediately.

Five to ten seconds after orgasm has taken place the clitoris returns to its position just above the entrance to the vagina again. Otherwise it takes about half an hour before everything inside a woman's body has returned to its unstimulated state; that is to say, *if* she has had an orgasm. If the woman has been stimulated without reaching the point of orgasm it may take longer.

Masters and Johnson relate that they had an opportunity of examining a prostitute who had had sexual intercourse with 27 men within a space of 6½ hours. She did not once have an orgasm (prostitutes very seldom do have with their clients) but did experience a certain amount of physical erotic stimulation.

Masters and Johnson then examined her for a further six hours during which time they observed that her pelvic muscles were abnormally tensed and swollen with blood and that they remained so right until the prostitute procured herself an orgasm by masturbating, whereupon all tension and blood vanished within 10 minutes.

In the man the most striking thing is that his erection disappears. This takes place in two stages: first, the penis decreases a little, quite rapidly, after which it slowly becomes smaller.

Masters and Johnson noted a very significant difference between the man and the woman.

When a man has had an orgasm he remains for a period of varying length utterly impervious to erotic stimulation. Masters and Johnson described this by saying that the man has a refractory period immediately after orgasm.

It is not only impossible to stimulate a man sexually, but as a rule any attempt to do so actually hurts or is most unpleasant.

In young or youngish men this refractory period is relatively short. After a pause, they are capable of having another orgasm. In older men this pause is longer.

For women the position is entirely different.

In the case of a woman, no such thing as a refractory period, during which she is impervious to stimulation, exists. If she is stimulated in the right way immediately after her orgasm, when her clitoris after a period of between 10 and 15 seconds has come up again, she is actually capable of having not only another orgasm but, in fortunate cases, even several more.

This is something we have not been sufficiently aware of before Masters and Johnson carried out their investigations. It has been said that some women were capable of having several small orgasms but Masters and Johnson have proved that it can in point of fact be a matter of several good orgasms and that the second or third orgasm is often described by women themselves as being the most intensive of all. Some women are capable of having as many as 10 or 12 orgasms and we have already mentioned the case of a 60-year-old woman who was able to have even more.

VARIOUS FORMS OF STIMULATION

There are various forms of stimulation which can lead to orgasm in a woman. For example:

1. She can quite simply get to the point of orgasm by allowing her imagination to run wild, in other words, quite literally without lifting a finger.

(This is very rare. Masters and Johnson did not find a single woman amongst all those who took part in their experiments who was capable of producing an orgasm just by indulging in flights of fancy.)

2. She can have an orgasm just by caressing her breasts, or if somebody else caresses her breasts.

3. She can have an orgasm by titillating her sexual organ (in particular the clitoris) – or if somebody else does it for her.

4. She can have an orgasm through ordinary sexual intercourse – in other words, with a penis inside her vagina.

A very important observation which Masters and Johnson made was that they were unable to note any difference whatsoever between the orgasms achieved through these various techniques (with the exception of method No. 1, but then they found nobody capable of applying this).

It is significant that Masters and Johnson observed all the reactions described above during the woman's four phases, no matter whether method No. 2, 3 or 4 was being used – and no matter whether the woman was alone or together with a partner.

They were, however, able to note that as a rule the orgasm was more intense when the woman herself was able to control the method of stimulation being used. In other words, it would appear that women are able to have a more intense, better orgasm by masturbating than with the help of another person. (Other investigations conducted on men's orgasms would seem to indicate that for them, too, orgasms achieved through masturbation are somewhat better than those resulting from ordinary sexual intercourse.)

We now know that during the woman's orgasm the womb contracts in the same way as during birth pains. The more intense the orgasm is, the greater the contraction. It is therefore very interesting to note that doctors never forbid masturbation during the latter part of pregnancy, despite the fact that masturbation would appear to have a much more intense effect on the womb than sexual intercourse.

SEXUAL FANTASIES

Masters and Johnson, just like earlier researchers, draw attention to the importance of sexual fantasies indulged in by women.

Most women have certain erotic daydreams which have an exciting effect. Unfortunately many women are shy and feel ashamed about these fantasies, but Masters and Johnson, and with them many other sexologists, strongly recommend women in particular to use these daydreams as an aid.

Other researchers have often described women who were able to have an orgasm solely with the help of erotic fantasies (just as in example No. 1).

Masters and Johnson do not deny that this may be the case. (There are also women who have orgasms in dreams,

24

but it can be difficult to determine whether or not they may have been doing something else besides dreaming.) Masters and Johnson were only able to note that even the most erotic of the 382 women taking part in their experiments were incapable of producing an orgasm solely with the help of the stimulation which sexual fantasies can give – at all events when they were being observed during the experiment.

As we say, it points to the fact that the phenomenon would appear to be rare, if it exists at all.

SEXUALITY DURING PREGNANCY

Masters and Johnson also conducted a special investigation of 101 pregnant women and their attitude to sex.

Here, once more, they came upon interesting material.

Most women reported that during the first three months of their pregnancy they were less interested in sex than before they became pregnant. This applied in particular to those who were pregnant for the first time.

But both those who were giving birth for the first time and those who had given birth previously were more interested in sex during the middle three months of their pregnancy. Most of them claimed that they were more interested in sex than they usually were when they weren't pregnant! Also, that their orgasms were better and more intense than when they were not pregnant.

During the last three months of pregnancy most of the women stated that their interest waned again.

Moreover, Masters and Johnson noted that the vagina becomes narrower during pregnancy because the swelling which takes place in the outer third of this organ during the plateau phase becomes more pronounced.

But it appears that the sexual climax reached by pregnant women is not quite so satisfying as that obtained when they are not pregnant – even though it seems more intense.

Masters and Johnson have not given a definitive answer

25

*This is an excellent position for intercourse during the latter
period of a pregnancy*

to the question of sexual intercourse during pregnancy.
But they have pointed out that only women who have a
tendency to miscarry need be careful about having
orgasms during the first three months of their pregnancy.
That is to say, not only through intercourse proper, but
perhaps in particular from masturbation. During the next
three months of pregnancy, the middle three months,
there would appear to be no reason to refrain from sex
or sexual intercourse. Nor would there appear to be any
reason to warn against lovemaking and sexual indulgence
during the seventh and eighth months.

But in cases where the doctor or midwife can detect
that the child's head has moved down to the neck of the
womb, there is reason to warn against making over-
violent thrusts during intercourse, thereby causing the
head of the penis to bump hard against the womb. In
these circumstances, it is probably best to refrain from
intercourse proper.

Cases are known of birth pains having started immediately after a woman had had an orgasm, but this has
taken place late in the ninth month when birth was expected to take place soon anyway. In other words, no
cases have been recorded of a child having been born
prematurely as a result of an orgasm.

There have also been cases of orgasm taking place
immediately before birth – orgasms which did not start

any birth pains. As mentioned above, Masters and Johnson do not give any definitive answer to the question as to how late in pregnancy is it safe to have intercourse. But they stress that many doctors have been far too cautious and, without justification for such excessive caution, forbidden couples to have intercourse. Masters and Johnson have found nothing to indicate that this is in any way risky for either mother or child during normal pregnancies.

Masters and Johnson's investigations also included women who resumed sexual relationships and intercourse proper with their husbands within a month of having given birth. The research team formed the opinion that in most cases these women felt sufficiently recovered already three to four weeks after birth, but that the woman *and her husband* immediately before and immediately after birth should discuss with the gynaecologist whether intercourse is advisable or not.

A number of woman, not the majority, are relatively uninterested in sex for a while after having given birth. But here Masters and Johnson have made yet another interesting observation.

Women who breast-feed their children appear to resume sexual activities faster than those who don't.

AN ORGASM HORMONE?

The idea is no doubt a little far-fetched, but there is something to it. Masters and Johnson noted that those women who breast-fed their children were quicker to show interest in resuming sexual activity than those in the group which did not breast-feed their children. Some of the breast-feeding mothers stated that the very act of suckling was a strong erotic stimulation.

It appeared that the sucking of the nipple by the child releases a hormone which presses milk out of the breast and at the same time causes the womb to contract.

Masters and Johnson reported three cases in which a woman had an orgasm while suckling her child. In a couple of instances, the reverse was also noted: that an orgasm resulted in milk running out of the breasts of women who were in the middle of a period of suckling.

So perhaps there is some important link or other between the hormone in question and orgasm.

In this connection Masters and Johnson also noted that a number of women had feelings of guilt about being erotically stimulated when suckling. Some stated quite

frankly that they didn't like suckling their child because it had an erotically stimulating effect on them.

Masters and Johnson stress that it is a pity these women feel this way. They should be able to enjoy the fact that suckling gives them a direct feeling of erotic pleasure. Possibly the phenomenon is one of Nature's cunning arrangements to make a mother particularly delighted to nurse her newborn child.

Or rather, *ought* to make her particularly delighted – if it weren't for the fact that we have so many cumbersome taboos on sexual feelings.

An attentive reader is bound to have noticed that we have mainly been writing about women and women's sexual reactions.

This is tied up with the fact that Nature has been unfair to women.

The majority of women have greater difficulty in having an orgasm than the majority of men.

In the following chapters we shall revert to how one can rectify this inequality, which is so patently unfair.

The way to derive
the greatest pleasure
from each other

Our entire culture is dominated by men and our sex culture by men's ideas of how women should be.

It is men who have created the myth about the sensual, passionate woman. In books, advertising media, plays and films men build up an over-sexed image of the ideal woman.

All ordinary, normal, warm-hearted, vigorous, lovely and sweet women can easily get inferiority complexes when their husbands insist on their living up to this ideal.

Individually, women walk around with the feeling of being frigid exceptions, because they have been led to believe that other women are so easily incensed to sexual activity. Men themselves believe in this myth and are all dissatisfied at their own rotten luck.

This can't be right!

Let's have a closer look at the situation.

THE FIRST TIME

In other words, it is very common for women to have inferiority complexes where sex is concerned.

It often begins with having heard or read about sex as being something simply marvellous. They have heard about the man's ability to lead women up to the very highest pinnacles of sensual delight, etc., etc.

30

Very often it is inferior kinds of pornographic literature or ordinary women's weeklies which cause women to foster such expectations.

Then comes the day (or night) when they go to bed with a man for the first time. The moment has seldom been particularly well prepared for. Often they are both confused. The man has not always had much previous experience. The woman as a rule is both frightened and shy, besides being scared of becoming pregnant.

It can hardly be termed a good basis on which to plunge into a satisfactory session of love-making.

One must also bear in mind that a woman's interest in sex, her desire to have intercourse with a man, is awakened much more slowly and much later than a man's. For this reason the first time she goes to bed with a man can often be a very great disappointment to her.

Most women imagine to themselves that all they need do is lie back and spread their legs apart and then this lovely thing, about which they've heard so much, will happen all by itself. But unfortunately it most certainly doesn't.

THE WOMAN MUST
HAVE A FEELING OF SECURITY

Nobody has told the young woman that she must know herself properly and have considerable confidence in her partner if she is to stand a chance of getting anything out of sexual intercourse.

On the other hand, the man doesn't always know so very much about women. A man assumes that since he himself thinks it is so wonderful to have his penis inside the woman's vagina, she must be just as delighted as he is. Many men believe that a woman's sensations of erotic pleasure are centred in her vagina, and that it is through stimulation of the vagina itself that a woman is brought to the point of orgasm.

Very few men have heard about the clitoris and not

even women themselves know very much about this little nerve centre. For scientific research has only just managed to confirm what skilful lovers have known and exploited throughout the ages.

SUDDENLY HE BECOMES
A COMPLETELY DIFFERENT PERSON

When a woman goes to bed with a man for the first time it is as a rule completely unplanned and improvised. And often unwished for on the part of the woman too.

It so happens that a woman can play erotically exciting little games and break off in the middle of them if she feels like it.

But nobody has told her that a man very quickly becomes so wild and excited that he simply cannot be stopped, that he becomes almost brutal in his persistency, with the result that the young woman is no longer able to recognize her hitherto sweet and considerate friend.

To her consternation she suddenly sees him as a demanding and ruthless creature bent on one thing, namely hopping into bed with her.

If she then gives in to him either because he forces her to do so, or in order to satisfy her own curiosity, she discovers that sexual intercourse seems to be a violent, perhaps slightly painful, but rather quick affair and not at all the lovely kind of experience she had expected.

In the majority of cases the man assumes that it has been just as lovely for her as it was for him. The most knowledgeable and considerate of them ask afterwards: 'Did you have a nice orgasm?' or, 'Did you come, too?' or some similar, faintly courteous remark.

MANY WOMEN PRETEND

After Van de Velde – the pioneer of sexual enlightenment in modern times – taught our fathers that a woman has a sex life too and that it is the man's duty to help the woman to have sexual feelings, some men exert a certain amount of pressure on women by insisting on their having an orgasm.

Not for the woman's sake, but in order to satisfy their own vanity.

For this reason many women answer, slightly frightened or confused: 'Yes, yes, it was lovely. You're really fantastic.' Sometimes also because they're scared of losing him.

Thus many women have got off to a bad start where sex is concerned. They have been deeply disappointed, sometimes even downright frightened.

Sometimes their menstruation then fails to come – and the reason may be precisely that they have been afraid this would happen. Then, on top of all the other disappointment, they have the fear of an unwanted pregnancy.

The fear of contracting a venereal disease can also help to make a woman's first experience of sexual intercourse (and subsequent experiences during the initial period) the very opposite of the romantic and lovely thing she has been led to expect.

ALMOST A SHOCK

It is almost a shock for a young woman to discover that neither she herself nor the young man react the way she had expected.

She is indignant at his egoism and lack of consideration, and shocked at her own inability to react sexually.

'I must be frigid – I must be abnormal,' she thinks.

She goes over all her feelings carefully and discovers that she does not derive any pleasure from sexual intercourse; on the contrary, she feels revulsion, disgust and disappointment.

She examines her own sexual organ and perhaps believes that she is deformed. Few women have seen the sexual organs of other women in full detail. Many have the most extraordinary ideas to the effect that they must be suffering from some deformity on this point. Utterly unfounded ideas, but none the less tormenting for all that.

Nobody has taught them that in precisely the same way that we all look a little different in the face and in the body there is also a difference in the sexual organs from one woman to the next, but that this difference plays no part in the degree of sexual pleasure that can be derived. The same things applies to the size and position of the clitoris.

Many men, too, have curious ideas about their sexual organs. Most men are convinced that their penis is too small.

Ignorant women, who feel deceived at having got so little out of sexual intercourse with their partner, may also think: 'Perhaps there's nothing wrong with me at all. Perhaps his penis is quite simply too small. Or perhaps I would have felt something if only he had been able to go on a little longer!'

IGNORANCE AND SUPERSTITION

All these worries are based on ignorance and superstition.

She is not deformed. She is not lacking in sexual feelings. His penis is not too small, and it wouldn't have helped even if he had been able to go on for hours on end.

All men are quite sufficiently equipped physically providing they have some knowledge of a woman's anatomy and the way her mind works.

(In parenthesis we may mention that the size of the penis is of no importance whatsoever when it comes to satisfying a woman sexually. The vagina can expand to permit the passage of a child during birth – and vice versa: during the plateau phase, just before orgasm takes place, the vagina becomes so narrow on account of the swelling caused by the afflux of blood that it can close

34

tightly round a pencil. No, that's not where the problem lies at all.)

Most women recover more or less after this first disappointment and resume sexual relationships with the man in question.

She may fall seriously and deeply in love with him and consider establishing a closer relationship, such as engagement or marriage.

The woman then discovers that she *can* actually react sexually, that she *does* feel something during the introductory manoeuvres, the so-called foreplay or love-play, but that she still does not manage to reach the culminating point of sexual activity known as orgasm.

Often she consoles herself that it will probably come all right as soon as they settle down and start living together properly, when they get their own home. But often her great expectations about marriage are not fulfilled either.

Time and again the woman will go to bed with her husband only to discover that the wonderful thing for which she keeps hoping simply does not come.

Soon she finds herself in the same situation as the person who, time and again, goes to a restaurant in the hope of satisfying his hunger. He reads the menu, makes his choice and leans back in cheerful anticipation while the table is being laid.

Then the waiter comes along and says that the kitchen has closed.

How often does one return to a place like this?

Actually, there's something rather touching, brave and dogged about a wife who time and again lies back in cheerful anticipation and says to herself: 'Now, *this* time! At last I'm going to achieve my objective! Now I'm going to experience this thing which people call marital bliss.'

Only to be disappointed again.

35

MEN DON'T HAVE AN
EASY TIME OF IT EITHER

Many men, in turn, are disappointed with the wife they have got themselves. She is not sensual enough, not sufficiently passionate. By heavens, he once knew a girl – *she* was sensual all right. Yes, good grief, he'd known girls who were simply *wild* about him!

These warm, sensual girls whom he once knew are now married too. And their husbands tell stories about girls whom *they* once knew and who, by heavens, were *so* passionate.

Dear Inge and Sten.

I am a young woman of 28. My problem is that my husband always wants me. When I'm reading the paper in the morning, when I'm washing up, when I'm . . . . .

I'm sorry my writing's getting a bit wobbly

Well, this is not only a joke, but also reflects a serious problem in many homes

It sounds as though getting married makes a woman less passionate. In a way, this is true.

During the first, exciting period when they each live in their respective homes, there are often long intervals between each session of love-making. One saves up one's needs for those rare meetings. Everything is new, exciting and promising. One is so expectant.

36

Later, these expectations are disappointed. The rather peaceful, often repeated sessions of love-making just don't lead to the joys the wife had hoped for.

In the beginning the man is patient, but now that they have become married he has increased his demands on several points. Now there is no longer any excuse.

One fine day he writes a little letter to his wife on her birthday – something along these lines:

My dearest darling wife,

Many happy returns of the day! When I look back at the year which has passed I find one thing most striking.

In the course of this year I have attempted to seduce you three hundred and sixty-five times.

I have succeeded thirty-six times. Every tenth day.

I have employed the time left over to note down the excuses you made for refusing me.

I've got a headache: Seven times.

It's too cold: Eleven times.

I've got a toothache: Twelve times.

It's too early: Fourteen times.

It's too hot: Fifteen times.

I've just been to the hairdresser's: Eighteen times.

It's too late, I'm too tired: Nineteen times.

Can't you see I'm washing up?: Twenty-two times.

We'll wake the children: Twenty-three times.

The window's open, the neighbours will hear us: Twenty-six times.

Not just now: Thirty-six times.

I've got a sore back: Fifty-nine times.

Don't you ever think of anything else?: A hundred and three times.

Dear, darling wife, don't you think you could try to find some new excuses during the coming year?

Your loving husband,

X.

Excuses of this kind are very common. Even women who have a completely satisfactory sex life tend to prevaricate and make excuses. It is as though they can't always remember that sex is lovely.

But of course it's much worse if the wife doesn't get anything out of her sexual relationship.

IT'S DANGEROUS TO PRETEND

Many women make a show of enthusiasm which they simply do not feel. Particularly at the commencement of a relationship it is easy to simulate out of consideration for the man, but once you've jumped on to this kind of merry-go-round it's difficult to hop off again.

If they have only been married for a couple of years, perhaps she can say gently to her husband: 'You know, I don't think I get quite as much out of our love-making as I might be able to.'

And then they can start talking the matter over frankly.

The situation is much worse if many years have been allowed to pass by. Men, as we have mentioned, are so vain when they're lying in a bed that it can be catastrophic to a marriage if they suddenly have the truth flung in their face: 'I've never felt a thing. I've just been pretending.' (Even if the woman has only done it to make her husband happy, so as not to hurt his feelings.)

In these circumstances it would probably be better if she said: 'I don't think I get quite so much out of it as I used to. Do you think we could try doing this? Or that?'

And then, slowly, guide him along the right path.

A PERFECTLY NORMAL PERSON

Yes, men are vain and easily hurt. And, of course, so are women too when it comes to a delicate matter like sexual capability. But tradition does not permit men to be human and weak. That is why their role is so much more difficult.

A man is expected to be big and tough. He is supposed to be tender, protective and shoulder the responsibility. A woman is supposed to be small and hesitant, almost like a daughter in relation to him. We accept these traditional roles from infancy – we almost drink them in with our mother's milk. From the time when we are very small we learn what a boy may do, what he may not do, what a girl may permit herself and what she may not. In films we never see heroes cry or who are weak in any way whatsoever. Short stories in magazines are always about strong, silent men who never pick their noses or need to change their underwear. It can be something of a shock to a young woman to discover that her husband is a perfectly normal human being. And of course if she only has short stories and films to go by she may not even realize that he *is* normal.

Here, the same rule applies again: In order to be able to understand each other we must know what is normal. It is not until we understand each other that we can relax together and start playing our traditional roles as hero and heroine.

WE MUST BE TOLERANT

In order to live together we must be able to overlook each other's faults. But all too many of us don't really like other people. We're suspicious and unfriendly. It is as though this unfriendliness is latent in all of us and only needs a very, very small amount of encouragement in order to come out.

It is so easy to slip into the attitude that all the others are peculiar and silly – it makes us feel ourselves to be just a little bit more important. It diminishes our own feeling of uncertainty.

And if we believe that we ourselves are abnormal or inadequate – which is something all too many people believe – we find a certain satisfaction in seeking out precisely the traits in our partner where he or she does not quite come up to scratch.

It's simple, it's tempting – but it cuts both ways, for it prevents us from having a lovely time.

HOW DOES ONE SATISFY A WOMAN?

If a man has got as far as asking how one satisfies a woman much has been won. It means that he has shelved his vanity, that he is ready to co-operate. But even that is not quite enough. There are a number of practical details which should be in order. If you're going to make love successfully you've got to have sufficient space as well as time.

A cosy little corner, plenty of time and nobody to come and disturb you sounds like dry and dull planning devoid of romance. But *is* it really? It is possible to look forward to a marvellous supper while you are out shopping for the ingredients. The joys of anticipation are wonderful too, and there is nothing wrong with planning a spot of love-making in the evening, or for a Sunday morning.

In the case of some women, their appetite is only aroused when they start eating. It may be necessary for the man to press her a little, to remind her how lovely it was the last time. Or, in the case of the reverse, persuade her that there is no need to let oneself be defeated by a failure.

It is extremely important to be able to talk things over. Very few of us are brought up to speak frankly about our sexual desires, but it can be learnt.

As a rule it is easier for the man and he can start, for example, by asking her what gives her the nicest feeling. It is not always that she knows, and her wishes and desires can vary from one time to the next. Perhaps she won't even dare to talk about it, in which case he will have to experiment.

PETTING

Here we must say a word or two about petting, which means every form of sexual caressing apart from actual intercourse.

The expression originated in America, where young women are renowned for permitting their boy-friends to go a long, long way, providing they stop short of actual coition.

Petting, however, is an excellent form of training for young people prior to commencing a proper sexual relationship, and in the case of married couples it can be a good alternative to resort to in various situations.

Through petting a woman and a man can get to know themselves and their partners. Both partners can, by means of skilful, imaginative petting, reach the point of orgasm. What is more, petting doesn't result in pregnancy.

The clitoris can be stimulated with the hand, the fingers, the tongue and in other ways without actually inserting the penis into the vagina.

In the same way a woman can caress the man's penis to the point of orgasm with her hands, fingers, mouth or whatever else they think up between them, still without actually inserting the penis into the vagina.

Many happily married couples admit that in the course of their love-play they employ many of the techniques classified as 'petting' in order to help the woman reach the point of orgasm. The point is, a woman doesn't always find it easy to have an orgasm so it should be more or less a case of 'no holds barred'.

THE CLITORIS – CENTRE
OF A WOMAN'S EROTIC SENSATIONS

The clitoris plays a very large role in connection with a woman's erotic sensations and sexual satisfaction, and the stimulation of this organ is the most reliable way of achieving an orgasm. Of course, this does not apply in all cases. Some women are capable of having an orgasm through stimulation of the vagina itself.

As we mentioned above, this can be stimulated with the fingers, the hand, the mouth or in any other way – for example, with an electric vibrator or the like, according to how relaxed and confident the woman feels. The clitoris is situated at the point where the smaller vaginal lips meet, and as a rule it is possible to find it by running your finger or tongue along the smaller vaginal lips until you reach it. Sometimes the woman will give a little jerk when you actually touch it.

The clitoris can be stimulated gently or firmly. Some women prefer the stimulation to be firm and constant to start with and gradually become gentler; others prefer things the other way round, and then again others prefer to switch backwards and forwards between hard and gentle stimulation. It requires patience and tact on the part of the man and the woman to achieve the best rhythm and intensity. Once in a while the woman must say quite clearly whether it is the way she likes it or not, and the man must not feel insulted if she says she would like to have a different kind of stimulation or if she wishes to help things along a little herself. Very often women find it difficult to tell men exactly how they would like things to be.

The clitoris consists of a shaft and a head just as in the case of the man's penis. The head is the most sensitive part. When orgasm is approaching, the clitoris 'withdraws from the game', so to speak, as we mentioned in the first chapter. The man should not attempt to fumble around in search of the clitoris, but instead concentrate stimulation on the region round the clitoris.

From the woman's point of view it is best if stimulation is continued until she reaches the point of orgasm. Many men believe perhaps that when a woman has had her orgasm she is completely finished, and this is not always exactly very encouraging for a man. But she is by no means finished. Even after orgasm has taken place it is possible to continue stimulation of the woman. She will then become excited again and may even have another orgasm, even if stimulation of the clitoris is interrupted and intercourse proper commences with the introduction of the penis into the vagina.

All this takes time. It is a more complicated business for a woman to achieve an orgasm than a man, but here, as in so many other spheres, practice makes perfect. A man can pick up several valuable tips if the woman will take the trouble to explain to him the technique she uses when she masturbates.

AND WHAT ABOUT THE MAN?

For a man it is different. As a rule he has no difficulty in achieving his orgasm. But if the woman is going to keep up with him, great demands are made on his patience. These demands, however, are not difficult to meet provided he doesn't let himself be misled by the old-fashioned definition of endurance and potency, namely, that the penis must be kept in erection as long as possible. The genuinely potent man realizes that there are many possibilities. In any case he realizes that it is unrealistic to start off a session of love-making by inserting his penis into the woman's vagina for as a rule it provides very little stimulation of the clitoris – if any at all.

He realizes the importance of an introductory period of love-play and takes his time. He knows that the normal thing, the commonest thing in a happy marriage, is that the man satisfies the woman first and refrains from inserting his penis into her vagina and achieving his own orgasm until she has had hers. Nor does he allow operations to come to a halt if he should have a premature ejaculation, but still continues to concentrate on helping the woman to achieve her orgasm.

YOUNG PEOPLE DON'T STAND
MANY CHANCES

It is easy to draw up ideal demands, details which must be in order if we are going to obtain the greatest possible pleasure from each other. But do we accept the consequences?

How many young people have a bed at their disposal when they want to make love? How many have homes that can be termed conducive to sexual intercourse?

Instead we hear, time and again, otherwise intelligent

43

people saying that everything will work out in due course. Everything has always worked out for young people.

In our society young people become sexually mature long before they are capable of standing on their own feet. Parents are anxious to see them get themselves an education and become happy and contented fellow citizens. But it is also part of our responsibility as parents to give them the chance of training themselves to become happy and contented sex partners. It is not enough to enlighten them, but just as important to recognize the fact that young people have sex lives too and should not be forced to manage as best they can in parks and on public staircases.

A LOVE-NEST

Of course things become somewhat easier when they get their own home. There they will have a chance – at any rate, in theory – of making practical and comfortable arrangements and giving themselves plenty of time. But even then things often go wrong. Many people regard it as more important to have a dining-room and a living-room than to have a room in which you can have a nice time with each other without the risk of being disturbed. Others, as a result of wide-spread housing shortages, are prevented from making adequate arrangements of this sort and obliged instead to send their children to the cinemas on Sunday afternoons. And even though it can be lovely to plan with each other to do something at such and such a time, it is monotonous always to have to renounce the pleasures of spontaneous whims.

LOVE-PLAY

The prelude to sexual intercourse, foreplay or love-play as it is often called, can be varied endlessly – though perhaps it may be necessary for the man to take the initiative when it comes to variations and experiments. Many women have a tendency to cling to a certain method, in

The majority of men dream of a burningly sensual woman, anxious to take the initiative. But when they actually meet one ...

accordance with the psychological precept which says that we like to return to something which has given us satisfaction before. If a couple, for example, have got into the habit of letting the man help the woman first to achieve an orgasm by stimulating her clitoris with his finger, she may not feel very much like changing over to having the stimulation performed with his mouth instead. Luckily enough there is the possibility of one thing or the other. Or both.

There are many pronounced individual differences. It is not until both feel confident in each other (this is to say, not only in sexual matters, but also as regards other aspects of life together) that there is a chance of their having the courage to tell their partner their innermost desires. When this happens one shouldn't allow oneself to be bowled over or be shocked by the other person's idiosyncrasies. Gradually one has to learn that when confronted with something new one must give oneself the chance to get to know it. It is perfectly easy to go just a little bit further than one really feels like doing. A woman does not become a worse kind of person just because she smears lipstick on her nipples, if her husband badly wants her to do so. And his masculinity needn't feel punctured if she says she would like to read something pornographic before they start, or perhaps during actual intercourse. If you are going to eat rissoles every day for the rest of your life, it is neither perverse nor unreasonable if you say you would like to have apple pie one day and cucumber the next.

ACTIVE/PASSIVE

We live in a patriarchal society. We have become accustomed to expect the man to be the invariably active partner, the one who always takes the initiative. This is quite unreasonable. Activity or passivity is not a fixed, immutable condition, but depends upon the situation. The roles which society has told us to play can perfectly well be changed, and the initiative to start making love must come from the person who wants to most, whether it is the woman or the man. Many men would like to see greater activity on the part of the woman, and this is something she can learn to do. Another thing is that some women have to concentrate so much on their own orgasm that everything else goes by the board. But gradually, as the woman becomes more mature, more confident about her orgasm, it becomes more natural for her to be both impulsive and active, to the delight of both.

AFTERWARDS

Many people neglect what one might call the 'post-lude', or epilogue – particularly if they have been jogging along in a marital rut for some years.

During the first period of infatuation it is perhaps a little easier to continue to show tenderness even after orgasm. But if one has settled down into a steady relationship, and is more or less confident of achieving regular sexual satisfaction, all too often the husband, and sometimes the wife too, will merely turn his back straight away and start snoring without giving a thought to the other person.

It is a shame not to take advantage of this moment of tenderness and relaxation in order to enjoy each other's presence – physical as well as mental. For many people, the quiet period following immediately after intercourse is just as important to their mental satisfaction as the orgasm is to the physical side of things.

THERE IS NO PATENT SOLUTION

It's no good trying to draw up fixed rules to define an ideal sexual relationship. It would also become rather boring. What we have described here is just a framework which one can alter or add to. The important thing between two people is mutual confidence, having the courage to talk to each other and being certain of the other person's understanding. One cannot change oneself completely, but one *can* change one's attitude. One can try to be open and playful, to vary one's approach and curb one's impatience. It is wonderful to be together and to be in love, but love alone isn't enough.

The sign of a good sexual relationship is that it can get better – and that it goes on getting better all the time.

A perfect sexual relationship does not exist nor would we wish it to, for it would soon become both sad and trivial to have to lie there night after night being perfect. It's much more inspiring to realize that one is making progress and that the two of you are developing together.

We think that *that* is when a sexual relationship may be termed a happy one.

What is normal
and what is
abnormal?

What is natural and what is unnatural? What is normal and what is abnormal? What is perverse and what is not perverse? What is human? What is harmful?

We know that Americans often cut their food with a knife and fork first – and that they put the knife down on the edge of the plate and eat with the fork alone.

We know that in large parts of the world they don't use knives and forks at all, but eat with chopsticks.

But we also know that there are many millions of us who use a knife and fork in a way which we think is nice. We feel confident and secure. We know what is done. We know the right way to eat.

We have seen our parents eat. They taught us how to hold a knife and fork: 'No, not like that! Hold it this way! Use your right hand! Push the knife backwards and forwards like a saw, don't just press!' etc., etc.

It makes us feel confident – though also slightly intolerant towards others who eat in a different way.

We so easily think: What *we* do is right. All the others are a little foolish.

Nobody would ever dream of forbidding children to see a nasty drawing like this

NOT KNOWING RESULTS
IN A LACK OF CONFIDENCE

When it's a question of table manners we are thus fairly calm and self-confident. We've learnt, we're masters of the situation.

When it comes to sexual relationships we are at once much more uncertain.

For, as is well known, there still exists a taboo on sex, on everything to do with our sex lives and sexual relations between two people.

The result of this taboo is that we don't know so very much about what other people do. We were not present when our father and mother put their arms lovingly about

49

But certain grown-up people would appear to have dedicated their lives to preventing other people from seeing a drawing like this!

each other and proceeded to enjoy themselves in the most intimate fashion. Some of us have perhaps taken our parents by surprise doing something which we did not quite understand. And some of us perhaps remember being told to make ourselves scarce because something was going to happen which we were not allowed to see.

Unlike young animals in the forest and on the farms, we have not been present every time the fully-grown males and females indulged in copulation.

Later, when it was our turn, when we ourselves felt we were old enough to have intimate relations with somebody of the other sex, we had had no previous opportunity to study how others set about it.

So we more or less dived into it head first – without knowing whether there was any water in the swimming pool and without being able to swim.

Attempts have been made to let new-born monkeys grow up without having any form of contact with other monkeys. No father or mother and brothers or sisters or playmates.

When the monkeys grew up they were put in amongst other adult monkeys and then observed.

It was obvious that the monkeys brought up in seclusion had normal sexual urges but they didn't have the slightest idea what they were supposed to do with the other monkeys. They were incapable of performing the act of copulation, and never learnt to do so later on either.

It is by no means certain that the ability to have a sex life is something we are born with

We human beings, however, are not quite so ignorant. At least we grow up together with other people, other children like ourselves as well as adults, and we learn to contact them even though we have very seldom seen much in the way of sexual contact. Little monkeys, as we have mentioned, watch adult monkeys copulating. And when they themselves grow up, they attempt to imitate what they have seen the grown-ups do.

The first time they engage in sexual intercourse it is often with an older and more experienced male or female who is capable of showing them what to do: 'No, not like that! Stop! Do this and that!'

HOW CAN WE LEARN?

In our Western culture it is the custom for young people to begin with other young people who are just as inexperienced as themselves.

There are people who suggest that we should be able to rectify this state of affairs a little by allowing older men to teach very young girls – and by allowing young men to serve an apprenticeship with older and more experienced women.

There are even people who preach that children should be allowed to watch their parents making love.

This is perhaps going too far. Nevertheless, we think that we are letting down our young people if we conceal from them our experiences in the sphere of the problems involved in sexual relationships and love.

It's not enough with the traditional form of sexual enlightenment, which merely tells young people that a baby comes out of its mother's tummy because father has squirted sperms up inside the mother's vagina.

Children must also learn something which goes by many names but which really only amounts to one thing, namely sex technique.

And we must also realize that seeing young people have been let down over a period of many generations, there are masses of people today of all ages who know astonishingly little.

Those of us who are now grown-up or old never had a chance of learning anything about what other people did either.

That is why we have a taboo on sex.

For this reason it is wrong of us to dismiss enlightenment about sex technique on the ground that it is the sort of thing any animal can manage.

Yes, animals can manage perhaps because they have never known any form of taboo. They show their sex lives quite openly.

Another objection one often hears runs like this: All these sex prophets are so busy blathering about sex technique they completely forget the spiritual side of love.

And the answer once more: There is no taboo on the spiritual side of love, on the side of love which is not sexual.

We can talk openly on the spiritual side of things. Here, we can all learn from each other.

IGNORANCE AND TOLERANCE

We have just seen that even if we know how other people eat, we are still intolerantly convinced that our way of eating is the only right way.

Even worse and more intolerant do we become when we pass over to the sexual side of our existence, which suffers from so much secretiveness and from so many taboos.

In the U.S.A. there are many laws concerning the correct way to behave sexually. Not that anybody knew anything about what was normal or abnormal, usual or unusual, when the laws were written, but presumably nobody dared to get up and protest.

Much later Professor Kinsey went round asking many thousands of Americans what they actually did. He asked

53

them questions about their sexual behaviour and about all sorts of other things that had hitherto been taboo.

It appears that, according to the laws in force at the time, about 90% of all Americans were sexual criminals. 90% of them admitted that they did, or had done, things which were strictly forbidden according to current American laws.

Dear reader! Now you've got to choose between two points of view:

1. The Americans are a lot of swine who ought to behave themselves according to their laws. They must mend their ways.

2. The laws are inhuman. The laws should be changed.

We have chosen to adopt standpoint No. 2.

But it is clear that the lawmakers didn't know enough about the sexual behaviour of human beings. That is why they were able to draw up laws or establish norms or rules which had absolutely nothing to do with the real pattern of human behaviour. Now and again they turned to the Bible for support and said: 'Here at least we have an authority which tells us quite clearly what we may and what we may not do.'

To this day, people will point to the Ten Commandments and say: 'These are the laws which God has given us.'

Let us examine some of them a little more closely.

THOU SHALT NOT
COVET THY NEIGHBOUR'S WIFE

Notice the way it is formulated: You mustn't have lustful feelings for your friends' and acquaintances' *wives*.

Modern scholars of the Bible can tell us that it was all part of the old patriarchal attitude among the Jews. I own my wife in precisely the same way that I own my cows. Nobody else may intrude upon what is my property.

But there was nothing wrong with having lustful desires for unmarried women who didn't belong to anyone. Even

... precisely in the same way as I own my cows

if you yourself were married. For your wife didn't own *you*, no more than your cows did.

REMEMBER THE SABBATH

We mustn't perform any work of any kind on Sundays and other public holidays.

There are people who still abide by this Commandment.

There are orthodox Jews who hire the services of a non-Jew to come along on Saturdays and light the gas for them, so that the previously-cooked food can be re-heated without it being necessary for the Jewish believer to do the work himself.

There is a story about some peasants who allowed a cow to drown in a marsh. They were unable to help it up themselves, because it was a Sunday and they couldn't work. It's all very logical. It is one of the Commandments in the Bible. The rest of us are perhaps not quite so con-sistent. We interpret the Bible in our own way and quietly disregard the most tedious Commandments.

Perhaps some people, for religious reasons, refrain from working on a Sunday. But they are very rarely so consistently logical about it as the orthodox Jews: they haven't the slighest objection to letting their women work in their homes on Sundays.

Modern people have thus abandoned the strict interpretation of the Bible because its laws are not human.

But we still drag a few illogical remnants of them around with us.

ONAN WAS PUT TO DEATH

The Bible tells us that Onan was put to death for what he did. (Genesis, Chapter 38, Verses 4 to 10.)

From Onan comes the term *onanism,* also known as self-abuse, or *masturbation.*

To masturbate means to give yourself some mechanical form of erotic stimulation.

A man or boy may rub and press his penis because it produces a pleasant sensation and, as a rule, leads to orgasm and ejaculation of semen.

A woman or a girl may in some way or other stimulate her sexual organ, in particular the clitoris. In this way she will often reach a sexual climax followed by a pleasant sensation of relaxation.

It is completely natural for boys and girls, women and men to stimulate themselves when the need has become so intense that it has to be satisfied.

It is just as common, normal and natural as the fact that we eat when we're hungry.

And it is just as useful as eating.

Owing to a misunderstanding in the Bible, masturbation has been condemned for generations.

MASTURBATION IS
NOT MENTIONED IN THE BIBLE

Those who read the Bible carefully will confirm that the whole story of Onan really has nothing whatsoever to do with masturbation.

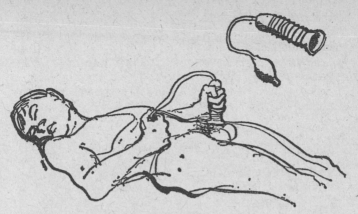

It is possible that some readers will be shocked by an illustration like this. But it is ridiculous to turn a blind eye to the fact that single people also have sexual urges at regular intervals. This and the following pictures show a few examples of more or less fanciful apparatuses, created by more or less fanciful inventors, designed to give pleasure to single men.
This apparatus can be placed over the man's penis, and then pumped up so that it closes tightly round it and then be used for masturbation purposes

An old Jewish law decreed that if a man died childless it was his brother's duty to 'procure' children for him.

The Jews were a small, weak people, and great importance was attached to becoming bigger and stronger, i.e. in increasing the population.

Onan's brother died childless. It was now Onan's duty (notice there is no consideration for Onan's wife's feelings in the matter) to make his brother's wife pregnant.

Onan was happy to go to bed with his brother's wife but for some reason or other he did not wish to make her pregnant. He therefore withdrew before ejaculating and 'spilled his seed on the ground'. In other words, the same form of contraception which we use even today in emergencies.

This was a clear transgression of a strict Jewish law. And it carried with it the demand for the death penalty.

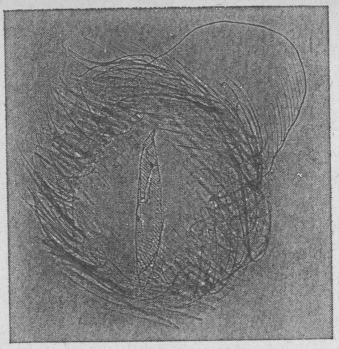

Another attempt to solve the lonely man's longing for a woman's body. A piece of plywood tube, a little rubber and a bit of rabbit fur

But it had nothing whatsoever to do with masturbation. Quite mistakenly, it was believed that Onan had masturbated and that this was his 'crime', whereupon the Church, Bible in hand, commenced to threaten perfectly normal, healthy people with all manner of hellfire, punishment and foul disease – right up to modern times.

And this misunderstanding, and superstition, has such deep and powerful roots that people even today have to fight their bad consciences over something which should not worry them in the slightest.

Here, using the same materials as in the previous picture, an attempt has been made to make a model of the lower half of a woman's torso. A number of people will find this revolting, shocking, ridiculous, humaliating – but the problem still remains. And for the lonely man, this can be better than no woman at all

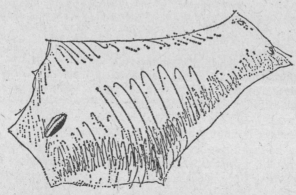

This is a Plagina (from the firm of Wapel Productions, Box 5728, Stockholm, Sweden). A pale pink female torso made out of plastic. But it is unreasonably expensive

This is the most fanciful gimmick we have as yet seen or heard speak of

The man is using a perfectly ordinary induction apparatus which is otherwise normally used for electrical experiments in schools. The current passes from a battery through the induction apparatus to a lead which he places on the foreskin of his penis. The other leads are attached to his nipples. The apparatus gives either a strong or a weak tingling, prickling sensation – which this man happens to need

This is not a picture of a perverted, depraved man, but of an unhappy, lonely, and frustrated person who has been forced to find something which hurts a little bit in order to cross the threshold towards his own sexual satisfaction

MASTURBATION IN LONELY PEOPLE

Today a great many of us have come so far as to be able to accept the fact that it is normal, natural and harmless to masturbate.

We are beginning to realize that young people and

children have a sexual need which has to be satisfied at regular intervals.

We are also just prepared to accept the fact that unmarried adults have sexual needs, and that it is not always possible to find somebody with whom to satisfy these needs. But we don't talk about it, because we still cannot believe that all human beings have sexual needs to a greater or lesser extent.

Our taboo on sex has the following result: If we look out through the window and see the passers-by we know they have sex lives of their own, but somehow we still don't really believe it. Don't worry, they have!

MASTURBATION IN MARRIAGE

We – that is to say, society – are prepared to stretch a point and accept masturbation as a childish form of satisfaction and perhaps also even accept the fact that it is resorted to by unmarried people. ·

But it is very obvious that we find it difficult to accept masturbation in a marriage.

We ourselves have received many letters from wives who have been beaten, ill-treated or scolded because their husbands discovered that they masturbated. Women have

We have even received letters from women whose husbands were most upset to discover that their wives masturbated in their sleep

written indignant letters to us saying that they have observed that their husbands masturbated and they have described it as beastly and perverse.

'Beastly' – well, that is an abused word. Because we human beings must on the one hand try to behave naturally, but we're not allowed to do so as naturally as animals.

Animals masturbate wherever they like, openly and with obvious pleasure.

But we're probably only allowed to do what is natural for human beings.

WHAT IS NATURAL FOR HUMAN BEINGS, THEN?

Owing to the fact that sex has been made the object of secrecy, it is difficult to determine precisely what is natural and what should therefore be permitted.

So long as society fails to acknowledge that the sexual urge is to be found in all human beings, married and unmarried, children, teenagers, elderly people and very old people – then misunderstandings are bound to arise.

The most important reasons why so many marriages crack up or are just poor is precisely the fact that two human beings, both equally ignorant as to what is natural and common in the sphere of sexual relationships, are forced to live together in a very restricted area.

It was not until Professor Kinsey and other modern sex researchers came on the scene that we at long last found firm ground under our feet when trying to judge what is natural, normal and common amongst human beings.

Many people assume that what they themselves feel to be right, natural and decent is the only right thing for everybody else. Thank heavens this is not the case.

It is just as wrong as looking down on those who eat with chopsticks.

Many mature women admit that in their sexual relationships they do things which when they were teen-agers they thought were quite dreadful – things which they at that time thought were unnatural, abnormal, and perverse.

Fortunately, they have changed their opinions. Others maintain stubbornly that sex and everything to do with sexual relationships is dirty and revolting. Their lives have not been enriched.

Not so long ago we received a letter from a wife who was at her wits' end and wrote: 'When I'm in bed with my husband I groan and scream. Because I do so enjoy it. But my husband tells me that I must keep my mouth shut. "Behave yourself like a lady", he says.'

This is deeply tragic. For the truth is that we simply cannot lie on our backs in bed and behave like ladies and gentlemen to each other. If we did, none of us would get anything out of our sexual relationships.

We sometimes hear it said that what is really necessary is a new code of sexual morals. This is wrong. The per-fectly ordinary rules for our behaviour not only in traffic but also in daily life serve perfectly well in the sphere of sexual relationships too. We must not harm or ill-use a person – nor, of course, in any sexual connection either.

BUT SURELY NOT EVERYTHING IS NORMAL?

Is there nothing which must be described as abnormal and perverse?

Here is a letter of this kind and our answer:

I am a young woman of 25. Not so long ago I was sitting on a bench in a railway station and waiting and directly opposite me was a young man who was sitting on another bench with both hands in his pockets.

As soon as he sat down he started to masturbate violently and at the same time stared straight at me. I tried to pretend to take no notice but after a while several other people sitting next to me saw what he was doing.

They began to move away and the expressions on their faces showed that they were extremely embarrassed and finally I became embarrassed too.

Afterwards I felt sorry for the young man. But shouldn't he have gone to a toilet to do this sort of thing? I masturbate myself but only when I'm alone.

I have never yet read an answer in your column in which you say that you feel anything is abnormal. In my opinion the young man at the railway station behaved abnormally.

Is there anything at all which can be called abnormal? I would so like to know.

Our answer ran as follows:

There are many things which we feel like replying. For example, take all these wonderful mini-skirts and sexy boots which girls wear nowadays, thereby filling poor men with the wildest of thoughts. Actually, don't you think it's rather abnormal that many more men don't sit down and get cracking?

No, of course, we don't quite mean that.

The young man did actually behave a little foolishly, a little provocatively, a little impractically in doing what you describe.

But we don't like the word ABNORMAL.

We all have our little idiosyncrasies which make us different from other people – also when it comes to the sphere of sexual relationships. But this does not make us either *perverse* or *abnormal*. Strictly speaking both these words only mean 'divergent' but now carry an unpleasant ring.

If two people prefer to make love in a chandelier and ask us: 'ARE WE ABNORMAL?' we would answer: 'It would be hard to suggest that many people share your tastes. But as long as you're careful you don't get 220 volts of dangerous AC current through you – and otherwise enjoy yourselves – we cannot really see that it is anybody's business but your own.

Are we abnormal?

'However, if you have got to the stage where you are only capable of performing in the chandelier, then we would suggest that you are accepting an unfortunate form of restriction of the possibilities of enjoyment to which everybody should have access.

'"He is ABNORMAL" – "They are PERVERSE" – these are horrid labels to paste on to anybody. The young man on the railway station bench with his clumsy manual labour and the couple in the chandelier are all three *divergent*, but if we call them *perverse* it immediately sounds much more accusing, doesn't it?'

WHAT IS PERVERSE?

Many women have accused their husbands of being beastly, perverse, abnormal.

'You never think of anything else,' is the usual phrase.

It is so common that it is well on the way to becoming normal.

It is less frequent that men accuse their wives of being perverse. But it does happen too.

What does *perverse* mean? Strictly speaking, it only means divergence from the average. And we probably all have our little idiosyncrasies, in the sphere of sex as well as in other matters. Is it perverse that some women ask their husbands to have a bath before coming to bed with them?

No, it's only very natural. But sometimes it is used as an excuse for avoiding sexual intercourse. In which case it is only a pretext. We human beings do tend to smell a little. But *old* dirt and sweat is more than one should be allowed to subject one's partner to.

If women were able to sniff at their sexual organs they would discover that they can never become so thoroughly clean as to be completely free of smell.

In other words, it is unnatural and over-romantic to attempt to quell one's own body odour – and the smell of one's sexual organs – with perfumes and other strange smells.

We are not suggesting that this can be used as an excuse for anyone to refrain from washing themselves. But it is meant as a kind of kick in the pants to those women who examine their newly-washed husbands, wrinkle their noses and say: 'You still smell!'

It is a human being's right to smell like a human being.

BUT WHAT IS PERVERSE, THEN?

In order to return to the question: What is perverse? we shall have to make two definitions.

1. You are perverse if you force, harm, or misuse another person in order to satisfy your own sexual lust.

It is a somewhat dangerous definition, for many women can abuse it and say: 'Look here, my friend, you're

The keyboard of sexual possibilities. We are all born with the
ability to play on all the keys. Society says that we must only
strum on a few of those in the middle. Some individuals are
stifled during their upbringing and are only able to play on a
few of the outermost keys to the right and to the left. Those
who are sexually happiest and most uncorrupted are probably
people who recognize the fact that they can (but don't necessarily
wish to) play on the entire keyboard. And conversely, it is
naturally worse if you cannot play on any of the most accepted
keys

forcing me to go to bed with you. You are demanding your rights, you are mis-using me. Therefore you are perverse!'

They are both right and wrong.

It is true that this is how they may see it. On the other hand, what happens all too often is that if the man does not press a little in a friendly, patient, but determined sort of way, then no development in the couple's sexual relationship will ever take place.

A woman's hesitation is often tied up with the fact that she has been disappointed in her sex life. She does not know sufficient about the correct sexual technique applicable to her particular case – and he knows even less about what can make a woman happy. Actually, both of them have a kind of duty to find out what other women and men are like.

It's just so terribly difficult to know where to start looking. Because there aren't so very many honest, easily-read books on the subject. The present book is an attempt to rectify this state of affairs. Because it demands a real effort to get down to the bare facts of what is human.

2. A person who only uses one of the hundreds of keys on the keyboard of sexual possibilities is perverse.

In saying this we are not suggesting that you are under any obligation to plunge into all sorts of experiments.

But we all have a certain duty to be prepared to try some experiment, something new.

As a rule it is easier for men. As we all know, they have very little trouble at all in reaching a sexual climax. And when you master something – and most men are actually masters of their own orgasm – then the desire to experiment comes along entirely by itself.

But where the majority of women are concerned quite a lot of work is required of them if they are to achieve an orgasm during sexual intercourse with a man. And if she has been fortunate enough to arrive at a form of sexual intercourse which now and again leads to orgasm for her it is understandable that she fights shy of experimentation.

It is understandable, yes, but she should force herself

68

to do it all the same. For her own sake, not just in order to make her husband happy.

Together they ought to try to find things which may give the woman an even quicker, easier, and deeper form of satisfaction.

It sounds so easy on paper. It's not at all easy in practice. But it is still a very important side of life. It deserves our putting more energy into it than we do in order to procure a car, a bungalow, or a boat.

WHAT DID PEOPLE DO BEFORE?

Let us go back in history and have a look at our forefathers.

We discover that there have been times, even in Scandinavia, when people had a much more liberal outlook on sex than we have today. And a very different one too.

There was a time, for example, when the whole family, including friends and acquaintances, would gather round the bridal bed in order to watch the bride and bridegroom make love for the first time.

Today we have a fear of nakedness. It is as though we had some kind of idea that the sight of a penis would cause harm to the eye of a woman or a child.

At any rate that is the way we behave.

Old church murals dating from about the year 1500 sometimes portray little old men piddling away into pots, but nowadays dreadful scenes like this have been decently covered up with a coat of whitewash.

In those days they didn't shock the congregation.

Were people unnatural then? Were priests and congregations perverse and beastly? No, they merely looked at things differently.

Perhaps their outlook was more sensible than ours.

We can also look at other nations and at the way their forefathers behaved in olden times.

When ancient Greece was at the height of its civilization, the Greeks did not have the panic-stricken fear of homosexuality that we have today.

In those days, a Greek might well be married and have children with his wife.

In addition he possibly visited a distinguished *hetaera*, a woman who was looked after by him and a couple of other men and with whom these men enjoyed themselves sexually. Finally, this same Greek might have sexual relations with a young man – possibly more than one. Nobody regarded him as perverse, abnormal, or beastly on this account.

The explanation is probably that we are all born bisexual. This means that we are actually capable of reacting sexually to both sexes.

However, as mentioned earlier in connection with the story of Onan, the Jewish nation at this time was very small and weak and its rulers were anxious to see as many children born as possible. For this reason Moses stressed the importance of heterosexuality and tried to combat homosexuality. The Jews were forbidden to become fond of persons of their own sex, because such relationships produced no children.

The first Christian authorities did not have the same strict views on the whole question of sexual relationships as the Christians of later times.

St Paul was one of the most assiduous denouncers of sexuality. But then he was also one of those expected to

'What obscene filth! Why do the police permit this sort of thing!' This is just another way of using your sexual energy

enter the Kingdom of Heaven at any time, so it is understandable that he attached less importance to sex.

However, for those of us who hope to live a nice long life here on earth, and who perhaps are not so sure about the Kingdom of Heaven, the main thing is to make our lives as rich as possible.

There are a great number of people who attempt to halt the process of development, who maintain that sexual relationships are dirty and that the naked body is ugly.

Some people devote their sexual energy to other things besides sexuality – namely, to becoming morally indignant and to drawing up regulations prohibiting this, that and the other thing.

Did you ever hear about the highly upset chartered accountant who wrote letters to the editor every week complaining that bathing suits were indecently small? On Sundays he used to drive out to the beaches in order to see whether his protests had borne fruit.

His agitation was sexual too – though of a very tiresome kind.

YOU HAVE TO WORK OUT
YOUR OWN ATTITUDE

The attitude which most people have to the question of sex is one which they have taken over uncritically from their forefathers.

And yet most of those who are now grown-up will state that they are dissatisfied with the form of sexual enlightenment which they received from their parents when younger.

But their disapproval is only very slight and few take the trouble to give their own children better enlightenment.

No, they have taken over, uncritically and without reflection, the attitudes of former generations. And it is temptingly convenient to do so.

It is most certainly true that fixed rules as to how things should be provide a sense of security. But it presupposes that these rules have been formulated in such a fashion that members of the community can abide by them.

To show how rules differ widely from one country to the next, we may mention that homosexuality between grown-ups is still forbidden in Germany and Norway, and that cousins are not allowed to marry each other in Finland.

In Denmark a new law is under preparation with the object of providing official recognition of a homosexual relationship as a form of marriage, of permitting a sexual relationship between a brother and a sister if the couple so wish, and of enabling those who choose to live together in one big communal family to receive an official stamp acknowledging the arrangement as legal and covering various aspects such as mutual responsibility, the right of inheritance and certain other practical matters.

We are not trying to persuade our readers to think the way we do. Nobody should assume uncritically anybody else's opinion about anything. We are just trying to stir the porridge of opinion a little and perhaps make some people so uncertain of themselves that they decide to abandon their *pre-conceived* notions and form their *own* opinions on the matter.

WHAT IS NATURAL?

Now we must have a glance at the animal kingdom again. Zoologists can tell us that a great many forms of obtaining sexual satisfaction exist amongst animals.

The various species have any number of possibilities of variation and even within a single species the forms of copulation may vary. That is why we should be careful before we start calling anything unnatural or perverse.

Why should Nature have imposed a particular degree of unimaginativeness on us human beings? Why should we not be allowed to cultivate our love lives in such a fashion that they become a series of exciting variations on the same theme?

Sometimes in the animal kingdom an animal would

appear to remain faithful to the same partner throughout its life. But it is not the rule.

Which means to say that many animals also have the possibility of varying with different partners.

But if we happen to have chosen marriage and faithfulness as a way of life, and if we wish to stand by our choice, we must create as many variations and innovations as possible within this monogamous form of relationship, otherwise we will run the risk of letting it become monotonous and boring for both partners.

It is true that many people will claim that women are monogamous by nature, but not men. And when men – but not women – have a little fling once in a while we tend to be lenient. The truth is that neither men nor women are disposed by nature or by instinct to remain faithful to the same partner for ever. In this respect there is no difference between them.

MAKING LOVE CAN
BE MANY DIFFERENT THINGS

The story is told about the members of a native tribe who were very surprised that white men lay on top of their women. The possibility had just never occurred to them. (Nor did the ancient Romans care very much for the position which we today call 'the natural position').

Incidentally, these natives promptly dubbed this position 'the missionary position'.

It seems they didn't find it so very normal.

In the Arab countries and in Asia it isn't the commonest position either.

The position one chooses should depend on how the woman is able to obtain the most satisfaction.

Kinsey was able to report that thousands of women who lay on their backs in the 'normal' position were in despair because they just didn't feel a thing.

There are a few women who are capable of reaching a sexual climax in the missionary position (the woman underneath and the man on top of her). There are also women who can get something out of making love when the penis is inserted from behind. In such cases it is sometimes necessary for the woman to stimulate the clitoris herself – or for the man to do so.

The man can also stimulate the woman's breasts, which some women, but by no means all, enjoy enormously.

The position which gives the woman a better chance of enjoying herself is when the man sits on a chair or lies on his back and she sits on top of him. Not that this is ideal either, but for the majority of women it is better than the two first positions mentioned.

We have received many letters from happily married couples who after years of experimentation have discovered that the most reliable way of ensuring that both obtain full satisfaction from making love is if the man first tickles the woman's clitoris with his mouth and tongue until she has an orgasm – after which he inserts his penis into her vagina until he reaches his sexual climax.

This sort of thing is not the slightest bit perverse, unnatural or unusual amongst couples who enjoy a happy sexual relationship.

Millions of married couples do something like this – or other inventive and imaginative things.

As a result of widespread ignorance these positions cannot be said to be used by the majority of people, but that doesn't make them either unnatural or perverse.

The most important thing is not to cling to a few misunderstood prejudices as to what is right or wrong. Admittedly more than half of all married couples continue to use the unimaginative 'missionary position' every time they make love. But then these couples also have the dullest sex lives. It is also amongst these couples that we find the greatest number of dissatisfied women.

AIDS ARE PERMITTED

There was a time when nobody used forks, because it was the will of God that food should be stuffed into the mouth with your fingers.

You weren't supposed to use a mackintosh or an umbrella either. For supposing God actually intended you to get wet? Women weren't given an anaesthetic when giving birth, because it was believed that a child should be born in pain.

Today, we all realize that it is unreasonable not to take advantage of any aid available.

But how many people understand that they can use aids today even when making love? How many married couples actually take the trouble to equip their beds for love-making? With cushions, bolsters, and something to push their feet against?

Or go even further and use massage machines, also called electric vibrators, which hum and tickle in the most delightful way?

An American doctor (who has been quoted by Kinsey, Masters and Johnson and other sexologists) has many women patients who complain about being frigid. 'I don't feel a thing, doctor.'

The doctor examines them and then places an electric vibrator on their clitoris. The woman's expression immediately reveals that she feels a great deal. She admits as much. 'You claim you are frigid,' he says to the woman in question, 'that you do not have any sexual feelings at all. And yet you experienced an extraordinarily pleasant and powerful stimulation from this electric vibrator. I haven't kissed you, caressed you, or muttered sweet words in your ear. I haven't as much as lifted a finger. And yet

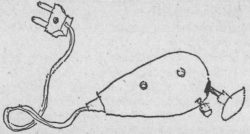

An example of an electric vibrator (Sanovit) with speed adjuster.
The apparatus is not heavy

you experience a very strong form of sexual stimulation. You are certainly not frigid.'

In the same way that one has to cross a meadow many times before you make a path, this American doctor believes that sexual sensitivity can be developed by training.

Other sex researchers, including Masters and Johnson, claim to have had good results with electric massage machines.

We too have had many cheerful letters from unmarried as well as married couples who have discovered the pleasant form of stimulation obtainable with an electric vibrator.

'But don't you grow dependent on machines of this kind? Are they not only for abnormal people?'

We have been asked this question so many times, and every time we answer NO. A couple's sex life becomes richer. The woman becomes more sensitive, she doesn't get so dependent – and it is not the slightest bit abnormal for a woman to need quite a vigorous form of stimulation.

'Won't my husband get jealous? Is he supposed to use it on me or am I to use it myself?' others have asked.

Yes, some men become jealous, because they happen to be terribly vain and believe that they themselves hold a monopoly when it comes to arousing sexual excitement in their wives.

They become just as jealous as some women do when they discover their husbands like to look at pictures of nude women or read pornographic books.

But this is an intolerant attitude, which prevents both of them from deriving greater pleasure from their relationship.

And in the majority of cases it is probably best if the woman herself decides how much stimulation she wants.

Anything that two people can work out between themselves is 'permissible' provided it makes both partners happy. Or, if it provides pleasure for one partner and does not actually cause direct harm to the other. And there aren't so very many things that do.

A
lustful
gleam

Most normal, ordinary men very easily become sexually aroused. They very easily feel lustful – and they enjoy feeling lustful.

Men like looking at women. At lovely girls wearing next to nothing. At girls undressing. At naked girls. Otherwise there wouldn't be so many scantily dressed girls as eyecatchers in advertisements.

The majority of men deliberately seek out exciting things in order to feel sexually stimulated. Men buy books and periodicals with sexually stimulating contents, they go and watch strip-tease, pornographic films, etc., because they enjoy being sexually excited.

In his report on the sexual habits of the male Kinsey concluded with a small gleam in his eye that there didn't seem to be anything that wasn't capable of arousing a man sexually.

Vast sums are made by exploiting the simple fact that men like feeling lustful.

But if we read Kinsey in order to find out what has a stimulating effect on the normal woman we glean very little information. Women are more complicated. Those who are out to make money don't try to provide pornography for women. Attempts have been made, but without encouraging results, despite the fact that many people have argued that this sort of pornography should be available too. But even experts in the field have been groping in the dark without really knowing where to start. Even when somebody hits on something or other, it soon appears that women are not so willing to buy. Perhaps because they just don't have the blatant desire to feel lustful that men have.

It is not primarily women who buy the illustrated weeklies filled with handsome, naked (or half-naked) men. They are bought – first and foremost – by men who like seeing pictures of other men.

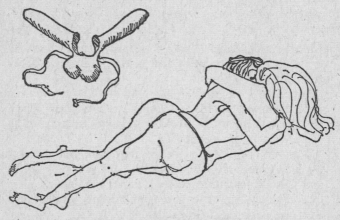

Here is a so-called 'pornographic' situation which both men and women find exciting: Two women caressing each other. But the double dummy penis in the left-hand corner, which can be fastened round the body, is something which to a greater extent arouses excitement in men. They believe that women cannot do without a penis. This is seldom the case

When women once in a while admit that certain things stir their blood a little, they usually mention pictures of naked or scantily dressed women – strip-tease with women, etc. – in other words, the same things that stimulate men sexually. But women don't buy them.

Many women admit that it can be quite exciting to see two women caressing each other – something which also

78

excites men. But women very seldom buy the periodicals or see the films which show scenes of this kind.

Naturally it is not quite fair to say that women have no desire to feel lustful. Perhaps we should modify the statement and say: Most women regret having no desire to be lustful.

Most women are able to experience a little of what they dream about in small glimpses on rare occasions. Fortunately the ability to react sexually increases slightly with the years – sometimes not until a woman gets into her forties, fifties, or sixties. (In other words, at a time when many men have given up and have written off their wives as hopeless cases. Such men are therefore making a grave error.)

AM I FRIGID?

The majority of women at some time or other in their lives have to face a struggle with the question: Am I cold, am I normal, am I frigid?

They have become disappointed in themselves and in their own sexual reactions – or, rather, lack of sexual reaction.

We have mentioned this before but it cannot be repeated often enough. There is no such thing as a frigid woman, there is no such thing as a woman who is completely incapable of reacting sexually.

But having said this much, we must add that there are women who have very strong sexual reactions – in other words, very sensual women – and less sensual women whose sexual reactions are weaker.

At this point the majority of female readers will think: Oh yes, I'm the sort of woman whose sexual reactions are weaker, I'm the less sensual type.

The majority of male readers will immediately think: That's just what my wife is, one of the less sensual types.

These readers are all right in a way.

For women are very seldom so hotly sensual as they

79

themselves would like to be – or, as their husbands would like to see them.

Sensual girls are *very* rare. In other words, the majority of women are not sensual enough . . . ?

One moment! What exactly are we talking about? What sort of a yardstick are we using?

Sensual girls . . . as sensual as who? Not so sensual as . . . not sensual enough . . . as what or whom?

WE COMPARE WOMEN WITH MEN

As we all know, we live in a patriarchy, governed and directed by men and their viewpoints, and we therefore automatically use a *male yardstick*.

In reality we therefore say: Women are not as sensual *as men*. Women are seldom as interested in sex *as men are*. Women are not so easily aroused sexually *as men*. There are very few women who are as interested in sex as men usually are.

Of course, it would be lovely if both sexes were equally interested in sex – or showed equally little interest. But it is wrong to claim that the male yardstick is the only right one.

It would be more correct to say that women are just not the same as men in this respect either.

It is normal for a woman not to be as interested in sex as a normal man – not to be as keen on making love as often as he is.

YOUNG WOMEN APPEAR
TO BE MORE SENSUAL

At this point, we must differentiate between young women and slightly older women because young women may sometimes appear to be a little more sensual. This is because so many young women have heard that sex is so lovely, so intoxicating and so wonderful. And so, for years on end, they remain in a state of cheerful anticipation, always hoping that *this* time, with *this* man, they will have this lovely experience they have heard so much about.

So in a way it is not so much a question of genuine sexual sensuality as of happy anticipation – which can create the same impression.

We know that women's sexual capacity and sexual reactions increase much more slowly than those of men. Men are most interested in sex between the ages of 15 and 25, whilst women broadly speaking do not reach their sexual peak until the age of 30 to 40. (Naturally, there are exceptions among men as well as women.)

The slightly older women who for a while have experienced a steadier relationship through being engaged or married have become more pessimistic and resigned. They have given up a little bit because they have so often had their hopes dashed.

It is true that older women's ability to react sexually has really become better and stronger with the years but all too often these women and their husbands have not succeeded in working out between them which buttons to press – which is essential if this increased ability is to be exploited.

AM I NORMAL?

It would be better if a woman between the age of 30 to 40 asked herself the question: Am I just as sensual as other women of my age? Have I the same ability to react sexually as other women of my age?

It's extremely difficult to get an answer to this question because we human beings are never completely frank with each other where such matters are concerned. Most people are afraid of being sexually inadequate, and either refuse to talk about sexual details, or else they boast and exaggerate a little to prevent other people from discovering anything.

Earlier in this book we established that a frigid woman

is a woman who simply does not react sexually in any way whatsoever.

So any woman who thinks she is abnormally cold where sex is concerned should ask herself the following questions:

1. Have I ever stimulated my sexual organ, brought myself to a sexual climax – i.e. masturbated? Have I ever felt any form of excitement in such cases? Yes or No?

2. Have I ever had sexual dreams, sexual fantasies, which have had a stimulating effect on me? Yes or No?

3. Have I ever, in any other way, experienced sexual interest or sexual excitement? Yes or No?

Even if a woman is only able to answer 'Yes' to one of these three questions we can quite definitely assure her that she is not frigid. But then we already know beforehand that frigid women do not exist. Despite this fact, many women are afraid of the stamp 'You are frigid'. Many men have – on account of thoughtlessness, disappointment, wounded vanity or for some other reason – flung in a woman's face the words: 'You are frigid!'

Just as if it were the pox, or some other disease.

AM I JUST AS SENSUAL AS OTHERS?

Most women are dissatisfied at the fact that they are not so interested in sex. They are not able, like a man (once again this comparison), to let themselves gradually become sexually excited just by giving their imagination free rein – or exploding with an outburst of sexual lust that comes over them like a sneeze.

It is normal for women to be sluggish in this respect. It is normal for women to forget that sex can be lovely (if they have managed to get this far with their husbands). When he says: 'It was nice, wasn't it!' with a happy, meaningful gleam in his eye, many women will answer – even those who do derive enjoyment from sexual relationships with their husbands: 'What are you talking about?' And they mean it, for they have somehow forgotten how lovely it was.

But unfortunately there is no getting away from the fact that the majority of women have not got as far as managing to have lovely times in bed with their husbands at regular intervals. Well, of course, they can have a nice time and become sexually aroused, and they can derive pleasure from seeing their husband have an orgasm. But the majority of women fail to have an orgasm themselves in the course of sexual intercourse with their husband.

On the other hand, most women know how to satisfy their sexual hunger alone. They are capable of masturbating until they reach the point of orgasm by stimulating their sexual organ. Often women also have extremely colourful erotic dreams in which various men do dreadful, but at the same time exciting and wonderful things to them.

Dreams of this kind, imaginative flights of fancy, are especially useful. Unfortunately many women try as hard as they can to forget them, endeavour to put them out of their minds. This is completely wrong.

Sexual fantasies, erotic flights of fancy or whatever one likes to call them are much better than hormone injections and many other things. Cheaper, better and pleasanter. It is precisely when she is making love with a man that a woman can find it of great help to *use* her imagination – let her imagination run wild on precisely the fantasies which happen to be particularly exciting and stimulating for her. It is a considerable help to all the other forms of stimulation which a woman needs if she is going to reach the point of orgasm.

DO I ACTUALLY HAVE AN ORGASM?

A few women ask in desperation: 'But what does an orgasm feel like? I'm not quite sure whether I have one or not.'

As a rule one is tempted to answer: 'If you're not sure

83

Many people have fantasies like this which they would never dream of realizing in practice. Many people, yes!

whether you have had an orgasm, you haven't had one!' To a certain extent this is right, because one is certainly in no doubt when an orgasm *does* come. But there may be something else behind the question. The woman may mean: 'Do I have the right kind of orgasm? Isn't there another, better kind?'

The question may arise from a serious misunderstanding.

It may arise because these women believe that an orgasm resulting from sexual intercourse or from petting in one form or another is a different kind of orgasm from the kind you get when you masturbate.

84

Probably more people than we choose to believe have, to a greater or lesser extent, masochistic or sadistic wishes of this kind

Slight tendencies of this kind may be said to belong within the bounds of what is normal

Some women believe that an orgasm produced by masturbating is one thing, the kind of orgasm you have in your dreams another, a clitoral orgasm a third form and that the fourth, the so-called vaginal orgasm (an orgasm produced by having the penis inside the vagina), is the best kind and the only right kind.

They've got it all wrong!

Masters and Johnson point out in their report on human sexual behaviour that there is only one kind of orgasm.

It can – particularly in the case of women – be felt deeply or not so deeply, as being small or large, and it can vary in intensity, but in all cases the same kind of orgasm is involved. The same thing happens physically and mentally.

As a rule, an orgasm produced through masturbation or in dreams is qualitatively better and more intense than even the best orgasm reached during ordinary sexual intercourse.

THERE IS NO SUCH
THING AS A VAGINAL ORGASM

Here we come to the stubborn myth which has embittered the lives of so many women, namely the myth, the superstition, about the existence of a particularly wonderful kind of orgasm which only occurs when the penis slides backwards and forwards in the vagina.

It cannot be emphasized strongly enough: *It is utter rubbish.*

There is no particular kind of orgasm which can be called a *vaginal orgasm.* There's only one kind of orgasm – even though it can be produced in various ways:

1. It can be produced if the woman stimulates her sexual organ either with her fingers or in some other way. She can also do it with an electric massage machine, with a telephone type shower in a bathroom, by tensing her thigh muscles with the help of a bolster or by any other method which happens to prove most satisfactory in her particular case.

Masters and Johnson mention the fact that no two women use precisely the same technique when masturbating. In other words, it is impossible to draw up any rules as to what is best or most satisfactory. Whatever a woman happens to have worked out is the best way in her particular case. And, as a rule, these orgasms are the best.

2. A woman can have an orgasm by dreaming she is experiencing a particularly exciting situation. This method is rarer than masturbation, but these orgasms can be exceptionally good.

In very rare cases, some women may be able to produce

86

a good orgasm by using their imaginations in a completely conscious state.

3. An orgasm can be produced while making love to another person (a) if the woman stimulates herself until she reaches a climax, (b) if the other person stimulates her, or (c) if they both do so.

(a) If she stimulates herself it will be more or less in the same way as in (1). Now she merely happens to do so in the company of another person. The presence of another person may have a slightly disturbing effect, but the positive thing is that human beings – apart from the need to satisfy their sexual urges – also experience the need to be together with another person precisely on this sort of occasion.

(b) If she is stimulated by her partner, it may be with the help of a finger, the tongue – or with the help of a massage machine or some other mechanical aid.

(Some people react very violently at the thought of using any kind of apparatus in this sort of situation. The same people accept without question the need to use utensils when we eat, or cups or glasses or drinking straws when we drink. They are also perfectly happy to drive a car, ride a bicycle, or take the train instead of walking. They also employ any number of aids in other circumstances without giving the matter the slightest thought. 'You get there faster if you cycle,' they say. But when it comes to sexual relationships they frown at the mere suggestion of using the slightest form of mechanical aid – despite the fact that the majority of women experience considerable difficulty in reaching the point of orgasm under the primitive conditions normally offered them during sexual intercourse.)

(c) In a number of cases the woman is able to stimulate certain parts of her body while her partner stimulates others.

But whether we consider 1, 2, or 3, it is as a rule the woman's most sensitive spot, namely the clitoris, that needs stimulating.

The clitoris resembles a very small penis, but it is even

more sensitive than the penis of a man, because this little organ in the female has just as many if not more sensitive nerve-ends than a man's penis.

A man can have an orgasm in his sleep – without as much as touching his sexual organ. If he is sufficiently excited, a man can have an orgasm merely by having his testicles tugged at gently.

However, everybody knows that it is the man's penis – and in particular the tip of his penis – that is the centre of a man's erotic sensations.

TESTICULAR ORGASM BEST?

Nobody would dream of suggesting anything so grotesque as that a testicular orgasm – that is to say, one procured by tugging gently at the man's testicles – should be the best and even the only right kind of orgasm for a man. Everybody would say: Rubbish!

But it is precisely the same kind of rubbish to claim that a clitoral orgasm is in any way inferior and that a vaginal orgasm is the only right and wonderful kind.

The misunderstanding about the so-called vaginal orgasm has arisen because *men* think it is so wonderful to be inside a woman's vagina. They feel that their orgasm arises by the fact of the penis sliding backwards and forwards inside the woman's vagina. They judge by themselves and form the opinion, erroneously, that the woman must think it is wonderful too – and that her orgasm must also arise as a result of the movement of his penis in her vagina.

A WOMAN KNOWS NO BETTER

The woman allows herself to be persuaded by this insidious argument. She often believes that she too should feel a penis inside her vagina to be a perfectly wonderful experience.

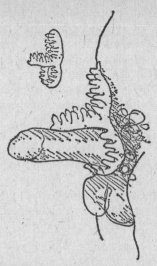

This apparatus is an attempt to help the woman. It is made of rubber and is supposed to be placed on the man's penis in order to stimulate the clitoris better during intercourse

Many different models and types are available. This particular one calls itself 'Happy End' and undoubtedly has a certain effect

But she seldom does.

In her disappointment she believes that she must be abnormal, cold, frigid – or something else equally dreadful. Often she doesn't even dare tell him about this – and if she does she runs the risk of his saying: 'Don't you feel anything? Don't you think it's wonderful? Then you must be abnormal!'

But it is perfectly normal and common.

The majority of women do not experience sexual intercourse as being particularly exciting. Quite simply because they have not been sufficiently stimulated by having the penis inside their vagina. The clitoris, the sensitive point in a woman, is situated quite a way from the vagina itself (just a little bit above the entrance to the vagina) and is very seldom sufficiently stimulated during normal intercourse.

It is true that there is a connection between the vagina and clitoris via the smaller vaginal lips. These are situated on either side of the entrance to the vagina and extend up to the prepuce, or foreskin, of the clitoris. As the penis moves backwards and forwards it pulls at the smaller vaginal lips, with the result that the foreskin on the clitoris is pulled backwards and forwards over the tip. But this form of stimulation is seldom enough.

(Most men will acknowledge that they feel a certain amount of stimulation if their testicles are gently tugged, because it causes the skin on the penis to be pulled backwards and forwards over the tip, though very few are capable of having an orgasm in this way. Most men would say, 'I would certainly prefer a more straightforward and direct stimulation of the tip of my penis.')

STIMULATE THE CLITORIS

So if one does not happen to belong to the very few who become sufficiently excited by this indirect form of influence being brought to bear on the clitoris – and who are perfectly satisfied with it – it is best to concentrate on the direct and more straightforward stimulation of the clitoris itself and the area surrounding it.

It is not until the woman has become fully competent and certain of her orgasm – and this can take many years – that she can begin to look forward to enjoying the many other sensations which are also lovely. Perhaps she has always wanted to have her breasts or her nipples stimulated – in which case she can try now – in combination with the stimulation of her clitoris. She may also begin to derive pleasure from the sensations she may feel in her vagina at the same time as her clitoris is being stimulated.

For of course women have sensations in other places besides the clitoris. There are many sensitive areas – varying somewhat from one woman to the next – which it can be advantageous to draw into their mutual caressing, particularly during foreplay.

At the same time as a woman finds it is becoming easier and easier to have an orgasm, she will as a rule discover that these orgasms also become better and better. The more skilful a woman becomes, the more areas she is able to draw into her general sexual stimulation at the same time as her clitoris is being stimulated. And the more areas of her body and sexual organs that are able to join in the fun, the better the orgasm becomes.

THE IMPORTANCE OF FOREPLAY

We've mentioned foreplay. Weighty tomes can be written (and have been) about the importance of foreplay, in particular to the woman.

It is extremely important for the woman to be warmed up slowly and thoroughly with every means at the man's disposal, both mentally and physically.

Very often the man judges by himself and says: 'Well, now, I feel like it and can ejaculate within a few minutes so if we give her five or ten minutes, I dare say it will be all right.'

It's wrong.

Broadly speaking, sexual foreplay for the normal woman does not last minutes, quarters of an hour, or half-hours – but *hours*.

It may sound both artificial and terrible but there is something to it.

The majority of women have to adjust themselves mentally for quite a long time to the fact that something is going to happen. It is this mental foreplay which takes time.

We believe that this mental foreplay also forms part of the definition of foreplay.

This is quite an ingenious idea to help 'warm up' a woman beforehand. It is actually an Asiatic invention. It is in the form of a wooden doll about 2 inches long. Inside the doll is a lead ball which rolls around and rattles. You are supposed to close the opening in the doll with a piece of sticking plaster and then place it inside a french letter together with a little ointment. The woman can then push this 'pre-warmer' up inside her vagina sometime before intercourse is likely to take place. It is therefore intended as an additional finesse to foreplay. This particular model was sent in by one of our readers

PAY HER SOME ATTENTION

It may sound banal but it is still a fact: Foreplay may start by the man coming home with flowers, a box of chocolates, or by showing some little form of attention. He can also be sweet and helpful and fix the lamp he has been promising to do something about for so long. Or he may also show his tenderness and attentiveness in some other way whether directly or indirectly.

During the initial period a man usually finds it quite natural to be attentive in this way. But as the relationship settles into a steady rhythm he tends to forget, because his wife becomes part of the inventory, just like the writing-desk or an armchair.

And so the first rule is: Court her!

Some men can do this sort of thing more imaginatively than others. But the important thing is to do it.

As if she were a stranger waiting to be wooed and won!

(Girls who already have good husbands like this, who are prepared to woo and win, should remember that men enjoy little attentions too. A favourite dish, a wife in a sweet dress – children who are not at home – just to mention a few examples.)

It is both partners' duty to remember that marriage is like a confined and rather uncomfortable little cupboard into which two persons, picked more or less at random, are pushed. Two people who were originally complete strangers and who, into the bargain, soon find themselves in the company of several other, less considerate members of the same family. If things are going to work out you've got to fight for it, incessantly and with all the inventiveness you can muster.

It may sound rather prosaic, but far too many women can claim that their husbands don't wash themselves properly.

A man who smells of old dirt and sweat is not particularly inspiring to a woman who manages to keep herself appetising and inviting.

We have spoken about it before, and drawn attention to the fact that it is sometimes used by a woman as an excuse for avoiding sexual contact – but part of the business of 'courtship' is that the man must remember to pay attention to this detail as well. And of course it is equally important for a woman to keep herself clean and fresh, especially round the 'crucial parts'.

DINING OUT – DANCING
– GOING TO THE CINEMA

In many cases, a woman's home is her place of work and her working hours are when she opens her eyes in the morning until she closes them again at night. Not concentrated work perhaps, but there are still things which have to be done the whole time.

Just imagine a woman turning up at her husband's place of work during working hours and making sexual demands! Surely it would be understandable if, in the middle of the act, he found his mind wandering on matters like: 'I wonder if Miss Carruthers remembered to write that letter to Binks and Binks Limited, in Manchester?' Or, 'I hope Johnson will turn up at the meeting with the P.R. people.'

The same applies to the woman's place of work: her home.

The man must therefore try to help her by removing factors likely to distract her.

If a woman is invited out for dinner at a restaurant it means she needn't worry about shopping, cooking, or washing-up.

In other words, this, too, is a way of being attentive.

Many women like going to see slightly romantic films. A tough Western, an amateurish, very direct pornographic film, or some kind of problem story is not always the best sort of thing to get a girl into the right mood.

A spot of dancing and music may prove much better.

All the things we have been talking about here come more or less under the heading of 'foreplay' from a woman's viewpoint.

And while we're trying to define foreplay we would like to extend the definition a little further.

A WOMAN'S ORGASM IS ALSO PART OF IT

Let us imagine that the man has been doing a spot of 'courtship' of the right kind and that the woman has gradually begun to get into the mood. She has accepted the fact that something sexual is going to happen, and now they're lying together in bed and are about to begin the foreplay proper, the little things which are going to bring forth direct sexual desire in the woman, the things which are going to excite her more and more until she reaches the plateau phase (see page 15) immediately before she reaches her actual climax.

We would like to extend the foreplay proper to include the woman's orgasm, her sexual culmination, or climax. Her orgasm thus forms a natural part of *his* foreplay.

The actual foreplay, the sexual togetherness which can lead the woman right up to the point of orgasm, can take 10, 20, 30 and even 40 minutes of intensive co-operation. Or more!

Many men like having the light on when making love, but this can be very distracting for the woman. It is a matter concerning which they must reach some form of agreement.

We have often stressed the fact that the woman must work in order to reach her climax, whilst the majority of men more or less have their orgasm handed to them on a platter – in fact, they are more likely to have difficulty in holding it back.

That is why it is best in the majority of cases if they both concentrate on helping the woman to reach her sexual climax with every means at their disposal.

Seeing that there are undoubtedly many women who have to work very hard in order to reach the point of sexual satisfaction, we would like to try to cast a little more light on the subject by putting things this way:

The woman must work both physically and mentally in order to reach a sexual climax, i.e. orgasm.

The physical work can be greatly reduced with the help of some mechanical aid, such as a vibrator.

In this way they will find they have more energy left over for the mental effort which an orgasm undeniably requires. And it is – as we have pointed out so often – a great help if the woman allows herself to indulge in sexual fantasies and daydreams whenever she is making love.

MEN ARE EXTRAORDINARILY VAIN

Men are often very vain when it comes to their own ability to make their wives happy in bed. They can't stand anybody giving them advice, nor the slightest suggestion that they should be in any way inadequate.

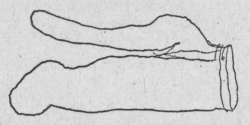

Another invention intended to stimulate the woman. A french letter with an extra 'rubber finger in the upper side. Possibly more of a curiosity than really effective? Sold by the name of Analibido

They get just as offended as an old-fashioned house-wife who believes that a vacuum-cleaner is an insinuation against her domestic prowess and therefore continues to sweep and beat the dirt away.

Where men are concerned it is tantamount to an attack on their honour as masculine he-men to suggest that it is permissible to use every form of aid in sex-play. We can easily manage without, they say.

It is a rather foolish and unbending attitude, but unfortunately the one adopted by most men.

But slowly, very slowly it begins to dawn on imaginative and intelligent lovers that the woman becomes more delighted with them if they permit her to use every available means of reaching the wonderful climax which men obtain effortlessly but which women have to fight for.

GOOD POSITIONS FOR MAKING LOVE

Many books on sexual enlightenment are full of the most imaginative positions which have one thing in common, namely that they are excellent during foreplay in order to work up sexual excitement in both partners.

Most of them are particularly exciting for the *man*, who normally does not need so much exciting anyway.

We are therefore going to concentrate on two positions which are particularly exciting for the woman – and which are excellent when it comes to helping a woman reach the objective of foreplay: orgasm.

All that is needed for the first position is a table, some cushions and a chair with arm-rests. You have to experiment a little until you find a table and chair that are just the right height.

The woman lies on her back on the table with her bottom almost right out at the edge and her feet resting on the arms of the chair. It is very important that she lies comfortably – plenty of cushions, by all means a mattress, and blankets or an eiderdown, in other words, whatever she likes best. It is important that she is able to rest her legs comfortably and relax on the arms of the chair, if necessary with cushions under her feet so that she can lie completely unconstrained.

The man sits down in the chair and makes himself comfortable with cushions at a good and suitable height. His arms rest on the table and can be used for various forms of extra stimulation according to the woman's wishes.

The actual stimulation is done by tickling the woman's clitoris and the area round the entrance to the vagina with movements of his tongue – gentle or hard according to the woman's instructions. As a rule she will object when it

When it comes to food, we are given detailed descriptions of all the ingredients in a recipe designed to make the enjoyment as great as possible. Spicy refinements are welcome and permitted

But when it is a question of an even more important field – describing positions for sexual intercourse which increase a woman's chance of satisfying her sexual desires – taboos still reign

This is not a recipe for a spicy or refined position for sexual intercourse. But it is a position which makes it possible for most women, with their husband's help, to satisfy their sexual hunger

feels wrong, but say nothing when it feels lovely and effective. He must be prepared to accept this.

The woman must help him to find the right rhythm, the right degree of hardness and intensity and the places which she derives most pleasure from having stimulated. Perhaps she will also like him to slip his fingers into the entrance of her vagina and thereby stimulate the outer third of the muscles of the vagina and the smaller vaginal lips. Or she may be interested in his stimulating the part behind the entrance to the vagina, round the anus, which is also richly provided with sensory nerves. Both man and woman must experiment until they achieve what they want. Wishes will gradually increase in accordance with the woman's sexual development. The important thing is that it is one of the surest methods for a woman to reach a sexual climax. Here it is as well to bear in mind that the woman's clitoris 'disappears' – more or less withdraws from the game – immediately before she reaches the point of orgasm. The man mustn't become confused by this and attempt to 'chase' the clitoris during this phase – this is important – but instead make his stimulation of the area broader and gentler. Not so very much stimulation is required at this point, because by now the whole area surrounding the entrance to the vagina will be very sensitive.

Once the woman has had her orgasm the man can get up and insert his penis in her vagina and have his own orgasm.

In the next position both the man and the woman lie down on a wide bed. She lies on her back with her legs apart and her knees slightly bent. He lies on her right-hand side, not next to her but at an angle of about 45 degrees, pushing himself in under her right leg so that the lower parts of their bodies meet. His right leg then passes up between her legs. In order to make it more comfortable she can support her right foot against the wall or the bed end. Her right leg will thus rest over his middle or hip, the knee bent. The position is comfortable

99

for both partners and the man will find it easy to get at what he wants both with his penis and one hand.

In this position the woman has the possibility of stimulating her clitoris and the area round her clitoris with her hand, her fingers – or with one of the electric vibrators which we recommend.

If the man is afraid of coming too quickly, of having his orgasm earlier than the woman, he need not insert his penis into her vagina until he notices that she is just about to have hers. Instead he can take part in the stimulation of the woman's sexual organs, breasts etc., according to her wishes.

This position offers the greatest possibility of achieving that very rare and wonderful thing which is called simultaneous orgasm.

It is an extremely comfortable position once both partners have experimented until they have found out what

Perhaps this is the most relaxed and best position for sexual intercourse of all. The woman lies on her back with her knees more or less bent up. The man lies on his side next to her with his right leg pushed between her legs and his penis under her bottom or inside her vagina

Both of them can moreover use their hands – and even an electric vibrator if they so choose. It is a comfortable position in which most people find they're happy to remain for quite a long time

suits them best. It is furthermore a good position for the lazy, during pregnancy, and for those who are in any way corpulent.

MASSAGE MACHINES

We have so often talked about these electric vibrators, stimulators, or whatever one likes to call them, which in reality have brought about such a revolution in the sex lives of many people that we feel that a little consumer information is called for at this point.

To start with, they are excellent for those who prefer to have lovely orgasms by themselves. In addition, they are extremely useful in the course of sex-play between two open-minded people who are bent on giving one another pleasure.

We may mention that authorities such as Le Mon Clark, Albert Ellis, C. L. Kelly, and Masters and Johnson warmly recommend the use of electric vibrators.

Many people believe, quite wrongly, that they are supposed to be used inside the vagina. They can be, if one feels like it, but the best form of stimulation is still once more the clitoris and the area surrounding it.

It is not without good reason that hundreds of thousands of such vibrators are now sold in Scandinavia.

Broadly speaking, there are two types, both of which can be used.

1. Massagers for plugging into a switch.
2. Battery-driven massagers.

The ones provided with a lead for plugging into a switch are the most expensive: about £6. The best ones are those on which the speed can be regulated, but most makes are satisfactory even if they aren't provided with this finesse. This type is usually supplied with a number of different vibrator heads which can be screwed on to the apparatus itself according to choice. One has to experiment, but the smaller vibrator heads usually prove the most effective.

The area round the clitoris, likewise the vibrator head (which is covered with leather, like a tiny cushion), should be smeared with cream or ointment to prevent two dry surfaces from rubbing against each other.

The apparatus should be as light as possible. After all, it has to be held in the hand for quite a while. A very

This woman is using a battery-driven electric vibrator which she uses to stimulate her clitoris and the area surrounding it

We have received many letters from women in their thirties, forties, and fifties who did not succeed in having a beautiful and relaxed sexual orgasm until they tried this method. A very marvellous experience

good, cheap, Swiss make with a one-year guarantee is sold under the name of SANOVIT.

The battery-driven massagers are as a rule more or less penis-shaped in order to indicate discreetly that they are intended for sexual use. But this should not lead anyone into believing that they function best inside a vagina.

They come in two sizes: the larger, heavier type is shaped like an over-dimensioned penis and costs about £2. Some of these have two speeds. The smaller type is about the size of a large lipstick and is naturally somewhat lighter, but on the other hand can be difficult to hold on to. However, a sheath – of chamois leather, for example – will usually solve this problem.

Potency
isn't
necessary

During the last twenty years we have received between 10,000 and 20,000 letters from people all over the world. Letters from women containing questions about themselves and their husbands – somewhat fewer letters from men about their own problems and those of their wives.

MEN HAVE NO PROBLEMS...?

Unfortunately, far too many men are inclined to dismiss their problems and claim that they have none. We have had many letters from women who complained that their husbands were much too smug and conceited. 'I have known many women,' these men say, 'and they have all been satisfied with me. Yes, downright grateful, in fact!'

However, the wives of these men aren't the slightest bit grateful, so there must be something wrong somewhere. The man's explanation is: 'Well, I've had bad luck. I've got myself a frigid wife, that's where the whole trouble lies.' But it cannot be right that so many men have all had the same kind of bad luck.

The explanation quite simply is that in the course of relatively short periods of acquaintanceship, women don't always get as far as giving up.

During the first years together, when they are very

much in love, the woman is thinking: 'It will probably come this time. This time going to bed with him is going to be the really lovely experience I've always heard it's meant to be.'

That is why women during these years seem to be happier, more affectionate, and even more grateful. Many women are also afraid of being abnormal, or else they are afraid of losing him. That is why they sometimes simulate delight which they simply do not feel at all in reality.

And men accept this, in a completely blue-eyed fashion.

Later in life they entertain their wives with stories about all the grateful girls they used to know in their youth. But in the meantime these very same grateful girls have also married and are disappointing *their* husbands by giving vent to their displeasure.

Unless their husbands happen to be the kind that have learnt something about women and sexual relationships.

IT'S GOT TO BE LEARNT

Many men surround themselves with a thick wall of defence if one suggests that they might be able to learn something about women and sexual relationships.

It is claimed that you can tell a man a lot of things to his face, but never that he is a lousy lover – and under no circumstances that he doesn't know how to drive a car. And yet women are supposed to be vain!

But even a man has to admit that it is necessary to learn to drive a car – at least necessary to acquire some basic knowledge about it.

Nobody would ever think of just putting two barely adult people into a car, starting the engine, putting it into gear, letting out the clutch and then just letting them drive off with the words: 'They're bound to work things out for themselves.'

No, they would obviously insist on their having an experienced instructor with them first who would be able to teach them the various functions of the car and help them to avoid possible catastrophe.

And this despite the fact that they have probably often seen others driving a car.

But when it comes to sexual relationships the older generation is irresponsible in an entirely different way.

What did we actually learn from our parents before we started driving in the heavy kind of traffic known as sexual relationships? Were we allowed to see experienced sex drivers first? Did we have an experienced person at our side the first time we were supposed to steer and handle traffic, the gears and the clutch?

This is by no means a poor picture of the situation when we, as youngsters, fell in love for the first time and were supposed to get to know each other a bit better.

If we were lucky we might have been given some information to the effect that a car has an engine which uses petrol ... forgive our harping on the same image! If we were lucky we had been told a little bit about how a baby comes out of mother's tummy, once father has planted his little seed inside and it has been allowed to grow there.

PUT UP YOUR HAND!

We would like to ask our male readers who do not agree with us to put up their hands. In other words, those readers who think they received completely adequate information and guidance from their parents, who quite honestly and genuinely are satisfied with the knowledge they had when they were about to start sexual relationships with a woman – whether in the form of living together properly or perhaps just a brief adventure.

Dear readers, look around you! Isn't it a sorry sight? No forest of raised hands! And if we are to be honest, we must admit that we ourselves have had to fight our way through many disappointments until we acquired the knowledge we have today.

The older generation let us down. They let us just drive on without proper knowledge, without practice, without any form of routine or the support which their own experience should have been.

The result is shaking. We only have to look around us. How many marriages do we know which are harmonious and completely satisfactory – as far as we can judge? Children born out of wedlock and venereal diseases are also some of the consequences.

We have gradually, laboriously, acquired a certain amount of knowledge – some of us. But – cross your heart – how much do you actually know about the research that has been done on sex during recent years?

In all other spheres we are ready to agree that you are never too old to learn more. Perhaps this applies to the sphere of sexual relationships too?

Why shouldn't it?

MY HUSBAND ISN'T AFFECTIONATE

Many women complain that their husbands find it difficult to express their feelings. Most women continue to be romantic. They appreciate a loving word, a little hug or a kiss now and then, but their husbands let them down in this respect.

Why?

We have spoken previously about the sexual role which men and women are forced into already as children: 'A girl doesn't understand technical things and mathematics. She is gentle and weeps easily.' Or: 'Big boys don't cry. They're tough, grit their teeth and never show their feelings.'

In our childhood we were told that girls and boys were supposed to be like this. And after the influence of decades most of us have accepted this pattern of behaviour.

Many women who complain about a husband who never showed his affections, at the same time told their sons that it was only mothers' darlings who cuddled and allowed themselves to be tender and loving.

Far too many people are still victims of this form of unconscious double-dealing.

THERE ARE TWO POSSIBILITIES

Most men grow up and obediently attempt to play the part of the masculine man. Most of them more or less succeed – at least outwardly.

In a marriage there are two possibilities. Either the man and the woman get to know each other so well that she discovers that he is not always and in all respects able to play the role of a masculine man. She may discover it after a few years of marriage or after many years. Unfortunately the woman seldom reacts by saying delightedly: 'How lovely. I've got a loving and sensitive husband.'

It may be a very small thing which suddenly causes him to topple down from his inhuman pedestal. Or it may come in one torrential rush which completely bowls the woman over.

As, for example, in this letter:

Suddenly my husband tells me that his highest wish is that I should hit him when we have sexual intercourse. He is supposed to be my disobedient little child and I'm to be a strict mama who punishes him.

I certainly try to do my best, but I don't like it. I'd like to have a grown-up man, not a blubbering baby.

I've lost all my feelings for him – or at any rate am in the process of doing so.

There are several thousand men in this country who feel precisely the same way as this man does; it's not *that* uncommon.

It may also happen – and this is the other possibility – that the man and the woman live together in a sort of father/daughter relationship, in which the man is so distant and superior that the woman fails to discover that her husband doesn't correspond to the established masculine ideal. This doesn't mean that the man *is* the he-man like heroes in cowboy films. It merely means that she has no chance of discovering that he is a perfectly normal human being.

Many women who have perhaps discovered that their husband does not correspond to their false ideal of masculinity, may perhaps wish that they could have a father/daughter relationship of this kind so that they could keep their illusions. But it's a false notion on which to attempt to build up a relationship. Sooner or later the balloon will be pricked – and the result may well be catastrophic.

'IT'S TOUGH BEING A MAN!'

We can also quote another letter which describes something which is a problem in many homes.

In a way we're very fond of each other in the course of daily life – in a way. But we've got one problem. We have heard about men who like playing the part of a servant for their wives, men who like walking round in women's clothes sometimes, without actually being homosexual. My husband is very fond of doing this, but it doesn't excite me in the least.

Sometimes I dig out a few bits of underwear and ask him to wash them for me. He likes it best if I actually *order* him to do so. And then he washes them, dressed in a pair of my panties and a slip.

Why can't I enjoy it, why don't I get excited seeing he loves it and loves me more than ever afterwards? It just leaves me completely cold – and the next day I feel so foolish and sort of out of gear.

(Once again we must mention in parenthesis that thousands of men in this country feel the same urges as this man. Some to a greater, some to a lesser degree.)

We have deliberately chosen a couple of not entirely common examples in order to show quite clearly how men can sometimes drop part of their masculine roles with something approaching convulsive violence. Not entirely common perhaps, but not by any means particularly unique or unusual either.

It is probably more usual for a woman to discover that her husband is no he-man by noticing that he starts sulking whenever things go wrong for him, cries when he is scolded by his boss, drinks in the crudest flattery about his manliness, boasts, etc.

It can be a serious shock to a woman to discover that her husband isn't the he-man she thought he was. She has seen Errol Flynn in films and knows that he never cried, never wanted to be spanked and it was never mentioned that he dreamt about walking round in ladies' panties. She has seen Humphrey Bogart stand in a door with a cigarette dangling from his lips. John Wayne is also always hard and uncompromising.

It was a hero like this she had dreamt of marrying.

And instead she has got a completely ordinary *human being*, with qualities like those all of us have, when we become sufficiently old to dare to acknowledge our wishes.

There are undoubtedly a number of women who will fail to recognize their husband from these descriptions. Let us put things in another way by repeating a much-quoted truism: Men seldom get beyond the age of 8 – at most 12 years – emotionally.

Many women will smile knowingly at this. Women are in many ways more grown up and mature than their husbands – and yet sometimes they are allowed to be little girls.

(In many ways, yes, if not all. Perhaps this should be stressed in order to be completely fair.) We are all unequally mature in various spheres. For example, a person can be extraordinarily mature in economic and social matters and at the same time be extremely immature in his or her emotional relationships.

Seeing that little boys are not allowed to train their

110

emotional life ('A big boy never cries'), are not allowed to practise consoling, taking somebody's hand, feeling tenderness for anybody (including not playing with dolls), their development in this sphere is brought to a halt already in infancy.

Many women will say: 'It is true that *my* husband is a big child, but I have met many men who were *men*.'

Dear ladies, do you know what the wives of these he-men are afraid of? That other women may discover that their he-men in reality are little boys!

DIFFERENT SEXES,
DIFFERENT EXPECTATIONS

All this is the result of the fact that human beings do not permit each other to be human. If two human beings are going to have a lovely time with each other, they must be able to relax completely when they are together. They must be able to rely on one another. They *must* be able to be honest – to be both ridiculous and desperate in front of each other, without having to pay any attention to the roles which society happens to have allocated to us (for it is completely different in other societies).

These roles are imposed upon us at such an early age that they act just like the deformed feet of small Chinese children in former times – i.e. they take on a permanent form which has been decided by society. They then exercise a considerable influence on the behaviour of both the man and the woman in the course of sexual relationships.

Quite a number of the problems between men and women arise because both sexes meet each other with such different expectations.

We often get letters from lonely women – spinsters, divorcees or widows – who write: 'I do so long for a man. It is so difficult to find anybody.' We get corresponding letters from men: 'I do so badly need a woman. Where can I find one?'

These tens of thousands of lonely men and women –

People meet – and various kinds of sweet music fill their hearts. A great number of the misunderstandings which arise between people may be due to the fact that both sexes meet each other with different expectations

why don't they find each other? It is often bound up with the fact that their needs are different.

Women want romance, attentiveness, tenderness, conversation, contact – and finally a husband. The man has more down-to-earth desires: a housekeeper and, above all, a bed-fellow.

These lonely souls meet all right, but the divergencies

in their expectations often result in their never really understanding each other.

THE IMPORTANCE OF PUBERTY
TO THE MAN

The little boy grows up and begins to be a man. At some time or other between the age of 10 and 15 he discovers that his penis occasionally becomes stiff. It has often been stiff before – even newborn baby boys can have erections. But he now discovers that if he rubs his penis he gets a greater sensation of pleasure – a mixture of pain and joy, which culminates in an orgasm and ejaculation. Some boys also experience the same thing in their dreams, so-called nocturnal emissions or 'wet dreams'.

Kinsey relates that about a third of the many thousands of Americans he interviewed remembered that as boys and young men they had masturbated together with other boys or young men. What a third remembers having done is neither abnormal nor unusual.

But all these experiences leave their mark on the grown man. It so happens that as a rule he was never told he was completely normal – and that what he did wasn't the slightest bit different from what the majority of other boys and young men did.

Many men have on some occasion or other been afraid of discovering that they were homosexual. They may have found themselves cherishing very warm feelings for a friend – another boy or a young man – and many young men have known periods during which they were afraid of girls and nervous in their company.

The truth is probably that none of us is born either homosexual or heterosexual, and that we are not pre-destined to be able to love only persons of the other sex, or only persons of our own.

Human beings – both men and women – in reality are born with the ability to react sexually towards both the one sex and the other – in other words, we are bi-sexual.

113

(Actually *multi-sexual.*) But once again society forces us to behave in a certain way: men are only allowed to become fond of women – and women are only allowed to become fond of men. If a man discovers that he *also* likes persons of his own sex, society pushes him unmercifully out of the so-called 'normal' group and stamps him as *homosexual,* even if the better word would be bi-sexual.

If society discovers some well-known personality spending a lot of time with a person of the same sex, he or she is at once stamped as homosexual – or lesbian – even if it is a fact that the majority of homosexuals can fall in love with both sexes.'

Society is so strict in these matters that the majority of men react very violently and with something approaching hysterical fear when they as much as hear the word homosexuality. Women have a slightly easier time of it. Society does not regard the emotional life of women so sternly. Girls are allowed to dance with each other, caress each other – in fact, are allowed to behave in a far more bi-sexual fashion than men. As a result the majority of mature women who dare to be honest with themselves will also dare to admit that the thought of a sexual relationship with another woman would not be entirely foreign to them.

Men avow their revulsion so violently that it almost becomes suspicious. It is as though they (which means society) have built up a hard shell around these feelings. And under no circumstances must anybody ever be allowed to crack this shell. After all, men are tough, aren't they?

And homosexuals are just a lot of milk-sops – that's what people believe. But many men would be shocked if they knew that several of our best known he-men (for example, amongst Hollywood's film stars) have also had sexual experiences with persons of their own sex.

Many feelings of this kind take firm root during puberty.

It has often been said that when it comes to our sex lives, we human beings don't have so many opportunities of observing each other. We carefully conceal our own appearances from everybody else.

One of the points where this secretiveness tends to create problems is when a young man begins to study his own sexual organs. Most women, too, believe for a while that they are abnormal physically, because they have no idea what other women's sexual organs look like at close hand.

'My penis is wonky,' a young man once wrote to us, 'presumably because I have masturbated so much. I'll never dare to show myself to a girl naked.'

His worries were entirely unfounded. All men's penises are 'wonky'. This is something every tailor knows and he sews trousers accordingly: 'Do you dress left or right, sir?' Most men incline towards the left, the rest to the right – and it needn't cause anybody any concern. It has got absolutely nothing to do with masturbating. The fact that a boy or a man masturbates is completely normal – it even happens in the happiest of marriages – and it is both useful and harmless. And it cannot cause any damage – as so many people believe. Nor can it be 'overdone'.

(Of course it is obvious that you can eat so many cakes that finally your stomach bursts. And it is equally obvious that you would kill yourself if you tried to run from London to Manchester and back without stopping. In both cases it would be overdoing things – but who warns us not to do these things? Nobody does, quite simply because nobody would dream of eating so many cakes or running so far. A human being is capable of regulating himself. In precisely the same way, people don't masturbate any more than they themselves know they can tolerate. Some people masturbate perhaps five, ten or twenty times a day – others only once a day or perhaps every other day – but whatever they do is normal for the person in question, and there is no cause whatsoever to raise an admonitory forefinger and say: 'You are overdoing things.' For it is our desires which drive us forward, and desire is what regulates this sort of thing in each individual person.)

Thus nobody's sexual organ can become deformed through masturbation.

The majority of men believe that their penis is smaller than normal. They steal anxious glances at other men in changing rooms and then look down at themselves disconsolately. To start with, their worries are usually unfounded. It cannot be true that the *majority* of men have a penis which is *below* normal size! Secondly, Masters and Johnson relate that a small penis becomes much larger when it stiffens, and that a large penis only becomes slightly larger when it stiffens. Thus when filled with blood, in a stiff, sexually-aroused, erected state, the difference is not so great.

Thirdly – and this is the most important thing of all – the size of the penis is of no importance whatsoever to the woman. Furthermore, for the majority of women, the presence of a penis in the vagina plays a very small part in the degree of enjoyment they derive from intercourse. For the man, on the other hand, the sensation of the penis inside the vagina is much more rewarding, but we shall return to this later.

Many men have a superstitious notion to the effect that they can only have so many ejaculations in the course of a whole life. Figures like 4,000 and 10,000 have been bandied about. Thank heavens this is completely wrong.

There is no limit whatsoever to the number of orgasms a man can have. On the contrary, the more he has the more he is likely to have in the future.

The ability to react sexually in both the man and the woman can be compared with a muscle. Everybody knows that if you don't use a muscle it becomes weaker and is no longer able to do as much as it used to. And conversely, if a muscle is trained, it can perform much more. It is precisely the same with sexual ability.

116

WHAT IS POTENCY?

Potency means *ability*. To be *potent* means *to be able*. *Impotence* and *impotent* thus mean failure of ability, not being able to do something. Not being able to do *what*?

Be able to satisfy a woman sexually.

So much superstition and so many misunderstandings exist around this question. Previously one thought that if a man was unable to have an erection – if his penis would not become stiff – then he must be impotent.

And the mere fear of not being able to present an erected penis has paralysed many men.

For the mechanism which regulates this is very, very sensitive to anxiety and other emotional states. And both men and women have erroneously believed that everything depended upon the man's ability to have a big, stiff penis.

It has even been believed – and many people continue to do so – that a potent man is a man who can get a big erection and who can continue to have a big erection for a very long time, a man who is able to continue thrusting his big penis in and out of a woman's vagina for a very long time without having an orgasm, i.e. without ejaculating.

As we know, women find it much more difficult to achieve their orgasms.

Therefore it is understandable – but completely wrong – that so many women have believed that if only their husbands were able to go on and on with the normal form of intercourse, then their own climax, their orgasm, would be ensured.

It is thus completely wrong, because the action of the penis sliding in and out of the vagina very seldom stimulates the clitoris and the area round the clitoris sufficiently (as we have said before and described at length in the previous chapter).

A potent man is thus not a man who can get an erection. Nor is he a sexual athlete who can continue for hours

117

on end without having an ejaculation of semen. Nor is he a man with a particularly large penis.

THE MAN HIMSELF DERIVES
PLEASURE FROM HIS ERECTION

It is natural that a man derives pleasure from his erection for his *own* sake. Many nervous men, who have known their erection to fail as soon as they believed that the woman was demanding an erection of them, discover that there is nothing whatsoever the matter with their erection when it is only required to satisfy their own pleasure and sexual desires. Ninety-nine per cent of the patients who complain about a failing erection are completely cured

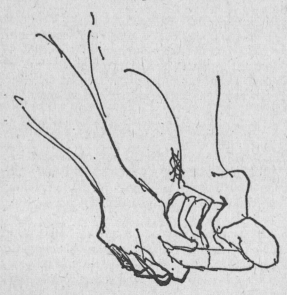

Here is one of the smaller – and cheaper – battery-driven electric stimulators. In this picture it is being used by a man under the tip – or glans – of his penis

when they discover that they are capable of satisfying any woman at all without using their penis.

In the other, very small group, in other words the one per cent of these patients who cannot be cured in this way, we find men who perhaps can only be sexually aroused by very special things, also men who have been angered or hurt and then become victims of a form of 'revenge' in that they find themselves incapable of being sexually aroused by the woman who has angered or hurt them.

Many of these men would be able to get a lot of pleasure out of using an electric vibrator. As a rule it is most effective on the underside of the head of the penis, the *glans*.

A BRIEF ERECTION

Some men have this problem: they can get an erection all right, but it won't last. It begins to droop again too soon.

As we have said, an erection means that the penis becomes filled with blood and thus firmer. The blood runs into the penis through veins which pass through the middle of the penis. The blood runs away from the penis through veins which lie just under the skin. So if the blood is prevented from running away from the penis by tightening something round the root, the erection can be made to last for a longer time.

It may sound a little dangerous, for of course we have all learnt that you mustn't stop the circulation of the blood. However, it doesn't do the slightest harm to tighten something round the root of the penis for a quarter of an hour or half an hour or even for a whole hour. We are not suggesting that you keep the thing lashed tight for hours on end. It should also be done in such a way that it can be loosened again easily and at a moment's notice.

It is unwise to do what some men have apparently done out of sheer playfulness, namely pushed their wedding ring over their soft penis and then let themselves have an erection. A wedding ring in this sort of position is something you can't get off by yourself. It has to be *sawn* off and it's not particularly funny.

You can use, for example, a silk ribbon or an elastic band and tighten it gently round the penis. One has to experiment. It's a good idea to place a little piece of ribbon or even a paper clip round whatever you have used to tighten round the penis. When the penis has swollen up and you want to loosen it again it's useful to be able to tug at this little piece of ribbon or the paper clip so that you can cut the ribbon or elastic band off easily with a pair of scissors.

There will no doubt be readers who will pull a face at these detailed instructions, but the problem can be a serious one for those who have found themselves in a vicious circle and who have lost faith in themselves. We would like to repeat that an erected penis is not particularly important to the pleasure a woman gets out of intercourse, but it can of course mean a great deal to a man. And in just the same way that many men are cured when they discover that their erection is immaterial to the woman's pleasure, many men become pacified when they discover that they are once more masters of the situation.

Many German firms advertise various miracle products – for example, creams or ointments which help to induce an erection. The most effective piece of advice is to be found in a German brochure, which either naively or very slyly says: 'The best results are obtained if it is the female partner who smears on the cream.'

We agree entirely. In the same way, the best results are obtained if it is the female partner who ties the rosette round the root of the penis.

And then we would add that warmth, sympathy, patience and helpfulness on the part of one's bed-fellow are better than all the creams, silk ribbons and elastic bands in the world.

But despite this, we know that something tightened round the root of the penis can help many men to overcome the feeling of powerlessness which seizes them when their penis will no longer 'do as it's told'.

And the mechanisms which govern a man's erection are to a great extent emotional, i.e. beyond the domain of sheer will-power – and, as we've already mentioned, they're very sensitive.

REPORT ON THE PUBIS RING

We have conducted a small experiment in Denmark. We asked for men who had difficulty with their erections to help us. Here is a report on the result of our experiments.

The pubis ring is a Danish invention. It is a small ring which can be tightened at the root of the penis and thus prevent the blood from running away from the penis again if there is a tendency for the erection to fail too soon.

First, we must emphasize that premature ejaculation is *not* the problem which the pubis ring attempts to solve. For in such cases the woman as a rule can still reach the point of orgasm provided the man continues stimulation with a finger, his tongue, or a vibrator. Then again, a man's erection will always decrease somewhat (or completely) after he has ejaculated. Admittedly, it may be presumed that the pubis ring to a certain extent may prevent the penis from diminishing in size after ejaculation, but – as we have already said – this is not the problem we are concerned with here.

The problem for a great many men, in particular elderly or old men, is that they simply don't get an erection at all – or that their erection is too slight for them to be able to insert the penis into the vagina – or that the erection disappears before they have managed to ejaculate.

In other words, it involves the sort of thing which either hinders or makes it difficult for the *man* to have an orgasm during ordinary sexual intercourse.

We asked for persons who were familiar with these

problems to help us by testing the pubis ring and reporting on the results they had obtained with it.

We sent out 10 pubis rings for testing and received reports from 9 men.

Furthermore, we received a letter from a rather upset gentleman who wrote that he and three of his friends had bought the invention, but that none of them had derived the slightest benefit from it. The gentleman in question warns us vehemently to stop cackling about the pubis ring and 'advertising an ineffective product' (X in table on page 124).

To this we can answer that we only recommend things

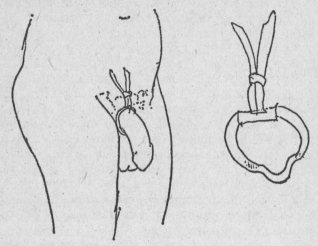

The pubis ring fits all sizes of penis. If you put some Vaseline on it a little dexterity will soon enable you to tighten it round the root of the penis by pulling at the tabs. In this way, the erection is supported because the blood is prevented from running out of the penis again

Afterwards, you can lift up the ring and loosen it so that you can get it off again. Obviously, one should not tighten it too much seeing that the penis becomes a little larger when you use it. But there's no need to be afraid that the ring may do any harm to the penis. After all, it only needs to be used for half an hour, or, at most, an hour

which we believe in – and that we do so entirely free of charge and solely in the interest of consumers.

Furthermore, we have received two letters from readers who have also bought the ring (A and B in table). This means that we have received reports from in all 11 persons plus the dissatisfied person who claimed to represent 4 persons.

We make no claim to be able to present a thorough and scientifically accurate report, but we hope that it may serve as an indication for those who have similar problems.

The report naturally has all the faults or weaknesses which arise when questionnaires are used and when there is no personal contact with the persons questioned.

We arranged the results in a kind of table and we quote a few of the letters which we have received. In this way readers can judge for themselves whether we have gone too far in drawing certain conclusions.

The original persons who agreed to take part in the experiment have been numbered from 1 to 9 – the two last buyers we will call A and B and the very dissatisfied buyer and his 3 comrades have been labelled W, X, Y, and Z. In other words, we have received detailed answers from 11 men plus 1 not-so-detailed answer from a gentleman who claims that he was speaking on behalf of 4 persons.

The experiment included men ranging in age from 39 to 75 years who have had difficulties with their erection for periods ranging from 1 year to 16 years. However, the majority of them are over 50 and have had trouble with their erection for a couple of years or less.

Four of the persons who took part in the experiment complained that it was rather difficult to keep the ring in place while tugging at the tabs. No. 5, moreover, wrote as follows: 'You have to pull it very hard in order to make it help – and even then it wasn't enough.'

One of those whose reaction was positive (No. 3) wrote: 'There is no harm in tightening it properly, because then it functions beautifully.'

Test person No.	1	2	3	4	5	6	7	8	9	A	B	W(+XYZ)
Present age	56	59		44	70	67	75	39	42	68	67	not stated
Married, unmarried or...?	unmarried	unmarried	married		married		unmarried		married	married	widower	not stated
Never erection?					very little		never					not stated
Semi-erection?				yes				yes		yes		not stated
Brief erection?	yes	yes	yes		yes	yes		yes	yes	yes	yes	
How long has erection been failing?	about 3 or 4 years	about 7 years	about 2 years	about 16 years	about 2 years	about 2 years	about 1 year	about 9 years	about 1 year	about 5 years	about 1 year	not stated
Was the ring difficult to tighten?	no	yes	no	yes	yes	yes	no	no	yes	no answer	no answer	
Did it help?	'a certain effect'	yes	'yes, just fine!'	yes	'no, not enough'	yes	no	no	yes	yes	yes	no

124

All in all, there were 6 persons who claimed that the pubis ring had quite definitely helped them. No. 3 wrote: 'Improved erection for far more than an hour.' A wrote: 'It has brought happiness into our marriage again. We had had five indescribably bad years.'

B wrote: 'Up to now have had intercourse three times using the pubis ring, each time with good results for both of us. Had a good erection which lasted for half an hour each time.'

Two of those who took part in the experiment, Nos. 1 and 5, were not satisfied. 'Perhaps a slight improvement is on its way,' wrote both No. 1 and No. 5. 'Perhaps it would help if it produced just slightly more of an erection.'

This is possibly also the explanation why the ring did not help for No. 7, who for the past year has had no erection at all.

We have included W in the table, but so much information is missing we don't feel we can trust his letter, the whole tone of which expresses dissatisfaction – also with us.

Result: All in all we can say – cautiously – that it seems that the pubis ring can help some people.

The idea of the pubis ring is to keep the blood in the penis once it has been pumped in and caused an erection. That is why it is easy to understand that it cannot help in cases when there has been no erection at all – or only a very weak one.

We are therefore prepared to recommend the pubis ring to persons who have semi-erections or erections which only last briefly. Not because we feel one hundred per cent certain that it will help, but only because we believe that there is a chance of its being able to help a failing erection.

(Perhaps we should add that in the rare cases in which the woman attaches great importance to having her orgasm with the penis inside her vagina – and where the man ejaculates too soon and wants to keep his erection after his own ejaculation – the pubis ring may also help a little.)

125

We have intentionally expressed ourselves with some reserve in order not to arouse false hopes.

The address of the inventor is:

L.J.J., Post Office Box 910, 2400 Copenhagen NV, Denmark.

The pubis ring costs about 25 Danish kroner (it may become a little cheaper if the demand increases) and you pay the postman for it when it comes. Otherwise it can be obtained from 'Maximo', Svaertegade, Copenhagen K.

Since the report was concluded two more letters have arrived. They are also positive; one of them is moreover a little 'happy end' story about a marriage which has only now become sexually happy. We must also mention a side-effect which several people have written to us about, namely that the tabs on the pubis ring provide an extra stimulation of the clitoris. Which of course is only an advantage.

COMING TOO QUICKLY

As we have said before it is usual for a man to ejaculate within less than two minutes once his penis is inside the woman's vagina.

We have mentioned that provided that the man sees to it that the woman has her orgasm *before* he inserts his penis into her vagina, then it's no real problem.

But some men come very quickly – and feel cheated. Other more experienced men are perhaps able to restrain themselves long enough for the woman to have a second or third orgasm after the first one (or even more).

If it so happens that the woman who has already had an orgasm feels excited by having the man's penis inside her vagina, there may also be a wish on the part of both of them for the man to hold back his orgasm, that he should be able to continue thrusting his penis in and out of the woman's vagina for a slightly longer time.

In such cases, something can be done about the problem too.

DEMANDS ON THE PART
OF THE WOMAN CAN BE PARALYSING

In the majority of cases it is the fact that the woman asks him to continue that tends to paralyse the man. If he believes that maintaining his erection and protracting intercourse for as long as possible is going to be of great importance to the woman, then the merest suspicion that she is making a demand upon him may cause him to ejaculate before he wants to.

For this reason it is only couples who are very experienced, skilful and well adjusted sexually who should experiment with satisfying the woman by means of the penis inside the vagina. As we say, it is best if the woman has had her first orgasm (or several) *first*, before any attempt is made to experiment with the penis inside the vagina.

PRACTICE MAKES PERFECT

Having made these reservations we would now like to mention a method which helps the man to delay his ejaculation once he has inserted his penis into the woman's vagina.

Dr Semans described in 1955 how a man can train himself to hold back his ejaculation. It is quite simple: the man (or his wife) commences to stimulate his penis until he comes very *close* to ejaculating. All men know very clearly when they are about to ejaculate. They are also able to give warning in such good time that the orgasm will not come provided stimulation is ceased immediately.

It is thus a question solely of stimulating the man and his penis. Both the man and the woman must be prepared to stop the moment the man indicates that he is very close to the point of ejaculation. A few minutes later, when the sensations have disappeared, stimulation can be recommenced, but care must be taken the whole time to stop as soon as ejaculation is felt to be approaching.

This may perhaps be repeated 3, 4, or 5 times a day for a week or so. If he wants to, the man may conclude each day by having a proper orgasm or normal intercourse once the exercise has been performed 3 or 4 times.

It should be remembered that even though the man is skilful about giving a sign when he feels ejaculation is approaching, he may miscalculate – and ejaculate all the same. If so, it doesn't matter. Just stop the exercises and start them again a couple of hours later – or the next morning. A few 'fiascos' of this kind don't harm the efficiency of the training procedures at all.

As a rule, within a very short time, the man will discover to his delight that he is now capable of continuing intercourse a little longer.

We must repeat that this method has got nothing to do with making the man capable of giving his wife an orgasm solely by means of movement of the penis in the vagina.

In the case of a great majority of women a much more direct form of stimulation of the clitoris is necessary in order to achieve this goal. But it can protract the enjoyment derived by the *man* from having his penis inside the woman's vagina.

And in the best marriages, where both partners achieve sexual satisfaction, the pleasure derived by one partner is also a source of pleasure to the other.

VAN DE VELDE

The great Dutch sexologist Dr van de Velde wrote his famous book on marriage (*The Perfect Marriage*) many, many years ago. It did an extraordinary amount of good and caused quite a justified sensation by telling husbands that their wives were entitled to derive some enjoyment from sexual intercourse too. Van de Velde made it a man's *duty* to procure his wife an orgasm.

This was important and quite right at the time when it was written, but it is a little dangerous to persist with this today seeing that most men now realize that it is only fair to help a woman to get something out of sexual intercourse too.

A tendency exists today to feel that a woman ought to have an orgasm in order not to disappoint her husband, not to wound his vanity. Her orgasm has become a kind of scalp which he can triumphantly hang on his belt.

Van de Velde's insistence on its being a man's duty to procure his wife an orgasm has become more or less a two-edged sword. As a result of it, far too many women have been forced into simulating a delight which they have not necessarily felt at all. If they didn't, their husband might become offended, his vanity might be wounded – in fact, he might even take his hat and go, angered at having been landed with such an ungrateful wife.

Today, we must revise van de Velde's revolutionary precepts somewhat. Not because they were wrong – they were necessary at the time in the light of the attitude and amount of knowledge prevalent amongst men in those days – but because (thank heavens) a great deal of progress has been made since then. Thanks to the steadily increasing emancipation of women, we would like to state that in our opinion it is no longer the *duty* of the man to satisfy his wife. It is the woman's *right* to procure herself an orgasm when having sexual intercourse with her husband.

As many people have possibly not got quite this far yet, let us modify the statement a little, and instead say: It is the duty of the husband to offer his wife the proper opportunities for obtaining sexual satisfaction. And it is her right and duty to accept the offer and, together with her husband, work out suitable methods.

It may sound terribly complicated and involved and of course in a way it is. This is because the majority of women have received an upbringing which prevents them from exploiting the possibilities offered to them. In the majority of cases a man will actually have to exercise a certain amount of stubborness, patience and gentle pressure in order to persuade his wife to take advantage of her rights.

And it is only during recent years that the majority of men have obtained access to the kind of *knowledge* about the normal sex lives of men and women which makes it possible for them to provide the right opportunities for women.

The husband is thus still, as van de Velde claimed, to a certain extent responsible for the amount of enjoyment which his wife obtains from sexual intercourse. On the other hand, this mustn't turn into a form of pressure on her, i.e. that she feels she must have an orgasm *for his sake*, to make *him* feel like a real he-man. An orgasm should be something which he teaches her to have for her own sake.

You're
never
too old

Women should know that, as far as men are concerned, their *ability*, their potency in the widest sense of the term, is a very sore point. And a man's potency also includes his ability to earn money and get on amongst other people, the make of car he owns, how he succeeds in his work – plus all the other things one expects of a man.

It is terribly easy for a woman to trample on a man's potency. 'Your car's always breaking down; it'll never start,' is just a simple and banal example of how a woman can betray her husband and expose him to the ridicule of others. We all know women who sometimes make their husbands look foolish and start criticizing them at parties.

'Are you really going to tell that silly story again?' she says, for example. She might just as well say: 'You're no good as a man!'

This kind of more or less thoughtless disloyalty is very dangerous in a marriage.

Of course the man must also be loyal to his wife. If he says: 'My mother's rissoles were a damn sight better than these,' or, 'My mother ran her house in a completely different way from this,' then he might just as well say: 'You're no good as a woman.'

Such little clashes often begin in bed, and often as a result of ignorance.

'You're frigid, that's what you are!' shouts the man in

his helplessness and ignorance. 'You come too quickly!' replies the woman who doesn't know a thing about it either.

Both of them know far too little about what a normal sex life entails and therefore start on a series of small 'digs' with the object of showing that the other is 'no good'. After a number of tiffs in bed they take their dissatisfaction along with them to the next party and start broadcasting the other's faults and wounding the other's vanity – until the wounds have become so deep that they can no longer be cured. Then the marriage has to be broken up or else merely continues as a kind of empty shell containing two lonely, hateful and unhappy people.

WHERE IS ONE SUPPOSED TO BEGIN?

If the wounds are still not too deep, i.e. if both are prepared to try to sort out the problems together, it is essential to get to the root of the trouble – which in all too many cases involves some form of defeat in bed.

Both the man and the woman must learn something about normal sex life. They must study and discuss the latest sexological results just as thoroughly or even more so than the theoretical things they have to learn in order to pass their driving test, for example. It is no good just skimming through a book or two and then saying: 'I didn't learn anything new, everything is hopeless.'

It is possible to learn something from even the worst books on sexual enlightenment provided one studies them thoroughly and attempts to form one's own opinion about one thing and another.

For a great many opinions are voiced in the latest books on sexual technique, and experts are far from always being in agreement. Despite this, no attentive reader can avoid learning one or two things he did not know before.

THE SIZE OF THE PENIS

Far too many men and women are concerned, for example, about the size of the penis (as we have mentioned before).

But it is entirely immaterial to the degree of sexual enjoyment obtained whether the man's penis is large or small. Masters and Johnson state quite clearly in their report that the fact that the woman is sexually happy and satisfied in her marriage is entirely independent of whether her husband has a large or a small penis.

Men with large penises can be poor lovers and men with very small penises can be fantastic lovers. Everything depends on whether the couple have managed to work out a satisfactory technique for their sexual intercourse.

This kind of *knowledge* can be obtained just by studying the latest books on sexology.

Not just the ordinary pornographic books. They may be excellent as appetizers and better than many hormone injections – particularly for men – but pornographic books do not deal with ordinary, normal men's and women's sex lives, desires and wishes. Pornographic books depict a false world of daydreams in which all the characters are glowing with excitement, beautiful, well equipped – and they all find it easy to do everything. From a literary point of view they are poor books, because they do not describe realities. And we may risk becoming dissatisfied with ourselves if we believe that others live in this way.

But if one has solid basic knowledge about the actual state of affairs, if one knows what is normal and common in the sex lives of other people, then it is possible to enjoy an ordinary pornographic novel for what it is: unreliable but stimulating romanticism.

ANOTHER EXAMPLE

The rule exists in our society that the majority of couples must be more or less the same age – the husband is usually a couple of years older.

With the knowledge we possess today about the sexual development of both the man and the woman it means that very often two young and more or less equally inexperienced people embark upon an emotional relationship without knowing very much about the practical details.

They start at a time when the woman, in most cases, has hardly begun to show any real interest in sex, whereas the man is at the height of his powers.

The woman is interested in kissing and cuddling, dancing and romance, whereas the man's sexual urges are stronger than ever.

In the majority of cases, this results in a series of defeats and fiascos and often ends with even the most patient man giving up after the lapse of a few years. He resigns. 'I've got myself a hopelessly frigid wife,' he says.

Then she reaches the age of 30 or 35, or perhaps 40, and by now has attained her sexual zenith. But then she hasn't been practising for quite a long time now. Her husband has given up and neither of them know sufficient about it. In a way, she is precisely at this time capable of reacting better sexually than ever before – but neither of them know it. At best, she now begins to make approaches to her husband, who merely reacts by becoming confused: 'What's all this now?'

With the years he has become slightly less interested in sex and simply cannot visualize his wife becoming aroused sexually – or that she could be aroused if only they both knew enough to pursue the matter.

If all couples knew something about the difference between the man's and the woman's sexual development the chance of mutual pleasure would be much greater. But none of us was born with this knowledge. It has to be acquired through study.

ANOTHER IMPORTANT POINT

Let us imagine that both the man and the woman have been studying the latest results of modern sexual research, that they are now at the commencement of a new epoch in their sex lives, that they are starting to apply in practice the new knowledge which they have gained.

The man will therefore have become aware of the fact that it is extraordinarily difficult for a woman to *say* when it feels lovely. If, for example, he has been skilfully and imaginatively stimulating the clitoris and the area round the clitoris, there is a risk of her forgetting to tell him that he *is* skilful, that it is effective and that her sexual excitement is rising.

She finds it easier to learn (but even this must be learnt too) to tell him when he does something wrong and stimulates too hard, too softly – or in the wrong place. But the majority of women have a kind of superstitious feeling that they will 'break the spell' if they have to say : 'That is lovely! Yes, that's right, that's just wonderful!' Women should try to praise anyway – even if it goes a little against the grain.

YOU'RE NEVER TOO OLD

The sign of a good marital relationship is that it gets better and better – and that it goes on getting better. None of us will ever achieve a perfect sex life – thank heavens. It's not much fun lying there being perfect together night after night – year in, year out.

All development takes place by fits and starts – and there are defeats, fiascos and periods of decline in between – but broadly speaking we become more and more skilful in our sex lives with the years. Even if our sexual *urges* decrease slightly.

The traditional picture of happiness is basically a false picture. Happiness doesn't mean floating permanently on a bit of fluffy pink cloud – completely without problems. On the contrary, it would be a hellish existence. But of course this is poor consolation for those who think their problems are insuperable.

Man is at the height of his abilities when he has problems to conquer. Not the insuperable and insoluble problems, but questions which are reasonably difficult to tackle and furthermore worth while fighting for. Happiness isn't a static condition – happiness is a constant form of movement with highs and lows. Nor is happiness an objective or a terminal station. Happiness is a way of travelling.

Marriage should not become a kind of idyllic duckpond. There should be room for several opinions, for a reasonable amount of disagreement is both healthy and invigorating. Living is solving problems. Living is feeling, thinking and having opinions – and the difference in views is merely stimulating. Living is also loving.

The kind of infatuation which one remembers from the first period of being in love is seldom to be found again in the course of a happy marriage. The excitement of being in love for the first time consisted to so very high a degree in the uncertainty and unsureness which one felt towards the object of one's love. 'Does she love me? Am I doing the right thing? I wonder if he will go on staying together with me? What does he really think about me?' etc., etc.

In a mature relationship you know each other and feel confident about each other's feelings. You can also continue to be in love with one another for certain periods, although without the uncertainty and unsureness – luckily. Sometimes the romantic aspect is neglected and it is often the man who does the neglecting. Possibly because it is not so important to him.

However, there is no law forbidding a woman to show little attentions to her husband. The man should try not to forget to be attentive; it turns old women into sweet young girls. When did you last give your wife a bunch of flowers? And when did you last think up a surprise for your husband?

Titanic passion is found even in happy marriages in

brief glimpses now and then – but sensuality lasts a lifetime. Also loyalty, comradeship and tenderness.

THE URGE NEVER
LEAVES YOU COMPLETELY

A young woman journalist once asked a 90-year-old authoress: 'When does a woman cease to be interested in sex?' The old lady blushed a little and then said: 'I'm afraid you'll have to ask somebody older than me that question.'

We never stop being interested in sex. Common to both men and women is the fact that the sexual urge never completely disappears. We continue to have erotic needs right until we close our eyes for the last time.

However, it is obvious that these urges are not as strong as when we were young. We just find that our desire to indulge in sexual activities doesn't manifest itself as often as when we were in our twenties, thirties, or forties.

Men are most interested in sex between the ages of 15 and 25, whereas the woman does not reach the zenith of her sexual desires until she is in her thirties or forties. But neither of the partners lose their sexual interests very much – and what one loses in the way of urges one wins in sexual experience, knowledge and confidence in each other.

About 50% of all women derive pleasure from sexual activities with their partners precisely in their thirties and forties, other not until they reach their fifties or sixties. There is no need to give up just because one is no longer so young. We know many examples of women who were 60 or so before they began to derive real pleasure from sexual activities.

Let us remember the female 'sexual athlete' whom Professor Kinsey and his colleagues encountered. Not that we want to give normal women inferiority complexes, just remind them of the fact that this woman, until she reached the age of 40, thought that she was frigid, because she had never felt anything sexually.

When Professor Kinsey met her she was 60 years old, had sailed past all her previously more skilful fellow women and was now able to achieve 20 orgasms in 20 minutes in the company of a man.

She was a unique case and there is no reason why we should let ourselves become blind with jealousy over her colossal sexual ability. The important thing is that sexual ability, to a greater or lesser extent, *can* be developed very late in life.

We have said that sexual urges do not make themselves felt quite as often when one has become older. There is another thing to be borne in mind: illness and other forms of debility diminish our interest in sex, and such conditions are naturally commoner when we are older.

But when the worst comes to the worst, there is still only the question of our sexual urges being decreased; they never vanish completely.

YOUR SEX LIFE NEEDS LOOKING AFTER

This is a lovely thing to know, because sex is something very central in the lives of all of us. We don't always think so when people pass us in the street and when we meet them in shops, but the policeman, the ladies' hairdresser, the grocer and the old people at the home for the aged all have their own little sex lives which are important to them – or ought to be.

Sex is one of the things which to a very high degree make our lives richer. So it is almost our duty to look after it, refine it, and generally care for it imaginatively and with the will to train and practise.

Masturbation quite simply helps to keep one's sex life going. It is important to young and old alike, to single as well as married persons, to happy as well as unhappy ones.

It is important to know that masturbation is *in no way*

wrong. Many letters which we receive from elderly people reveal that they have bad consciences because masturbation is a big problem for them. It shouldn't be at all.

It is healthy, instructive and lovely to masturbate; it also helps to develop our sex lives.

It is particularly important to stress this for the benefit of the many people who are completely alone, single people who have no one to be together with sexually, who have no sexual partner. Unfortunately a great many lonely people are married too, but for one reason or another they have given up sexual relations with their partner.

But masturbation can certainly occur in a happy marriage too. There is nothing wrong with masturbating just because one is married. In other words, masturbation forms a natural part of a natural sex life.

We all know that a cosy and festive meal together with a person one is fond of is one of the positive things in life. But this doesn't mean that we have to lie down and die of hunger just because for a brief or even longer period of time we are unable to eat together – for one reason or another. The meal you eat by yourself can be lovely too. An orgasm obtained through masturbation can be extremely satisfying.

So when married couples for one reason or another are deprived of the possibility of satisfying their sexual urges together, masturbation is an obvious and excellent solution.

It sometimes happens that men and women – who are married – feel like going to bed with persons they are not married to. This sort of thing can happen even in the happiest marriage, in which case masturbation while at the same time imagining oneself doing all sorts of lovely things with the exciting third party can be an excellent and wholly permissible form of unfaithfulness. One should merely refrain from entertaining the person one is married to with descriptions of these fantasies.

Giving one's imagination free rein and indulging in wild fantasies during sexual intercourse and masturbation is actually very, very important; particularly for women, but also for men. Scientists don't know so very much about it yet, but they are becoming aware of its significance as a sexual stimulant.

DIVIDE UP THAT DOUBLE BED!

It was recently reported from America that they are thinking of assigning the sum of $40,000 to finance an investigation of human snoring.

It may sound like a joke, but we know that it can be a big problem. During the past 20 years we have received many letters from women who complain about their husbands' snoring. Women snore too, but it appears to be much more irritating for a woman to listen to a snoring man.

Could it be because they are less satisfied sexually?

At all events it is a problem which touches on the question of the double bed, and sleeping in the same room.

In a way we can perfectly well understand the romantic notions which cause people to insist on wanting to sleep together. It sounds so cosy, so intimate and so wonderful to be able to snuggle up to each other and doze off in each other's arms.

Reality is more brutal. It is *seldom* particularly romantic to lie in bed breathing into each other's faces. Furthermore, one person may wish to read, while the other prefers to sleep.

In some cases, misplaced considerations of prestige are involved. Problems in connection with the housing shortage or personal economy cause people to feel that they must have a living-room and a bedroom. And, of course, to sleep in the living-room would be unthinkable. In other cases there may be a more or less conscious wish to keep an eye on the other person all round the clock.

But it is inhuman to be kept under observation night and day. In the end we shall find we can only be ourselves when we go to the lavatory. To be allowed to sleep alone in a separate room if one wants to is surely a basic human right.

If one's home is on the cramped side, even the kitchen can be used as a place to sleep in. The ideal thing is if either the man or wife – or both of them – have a bed large enough for two people to lie in when they are awake and want to have a nice time together.

Let us conclude our remarks on this question by saying, briefly, that you can't save a marriage by moving your beds together, by starting to sleep in the same room. But you may be able to save it by moving into your own, separate, rooms. Then both man and wife can snore and read and sleep whenever they like.

OLDER WOMEN – YOUNG MEN

Traditionally, men should preferably be slightly older than their wives.

Preferably...? Is this suggesting that it makes for the happiest marriages?

It is very usual for women in their thirties, forties, and fifties to find slightly younger, young and even very young men extremely attractive and charming. It can also be a very wonderful thing for a young man to have erotic experiences with a slightly older or even very much older woman – instead of with a girl of his own age whose sexual consciousness has barely been aroused yet.

Sometimes we get letters containing the question: 'I have fallen in love with a man who is 20 (or 5, 10, 15) years younger than myself. Everybody thinks it ridiculous of me to want to marry him, but we love each other and have a wonderful time together. What do you think?'

We answer every time that we, to start with, never understand why people are in such a hurry to get married. The first five years of a marriage are the most dangerous. The majority of people who divorce do so after a few years of marriage – so if it is possible to postpone having children and making one partner give up his or her job, we see no reason why people should plunge into marriage. It's better to start living together for a couple of years first and see how things go.

This actually applies to everybody – not just to older women who want to marry young men. It's no good trying to bind another person to you with chains. On the contrary. But having said this much we must also state that it is pure superstition to believe that there is any reason why a marriage between a young man and an older woman should not be a happy one.

One only has to look at things the other way round and consider some of one's married acquaintances. In cases where the difference in ages between man and wife is the generally 'accepted' one, in other words, where the man is 2 or 4 or 6 years older than his wife, how many of such marriages are happy?

The conclusion must be that if two people get on marvellously *now*, they should take advantage of the fact and be happy. The happy years which two people have had together can never be taken away from them again.

We often get letters from young people who are upset by the fact that their old widowed mother or father is considering getting married again. They become particularly upset if the parent in question has been left alone relatively recently, or if the person he or she is thinking of marrying happens to be much younger. Very often the children, even if they happen to be grown-up and have children of their own, display open animosity towards the new partners.

This is a terribly egoistic and intolerant attitude which only shows how little such children know about the vital force of love and sexuality. Young people consider they have the right to choose a mate for life without interference from their parents – and furthermore regard it as their right to receive their parents' blessing regardless of their choice. Old people should have the same right to love, choose – and receive their children's blessing.

Incidentally, there is a rule of thumb which says that the better a marriage has been, the shorter will be the period of mourning and the greater the chance the survivor will have of finding new happiness with a new partner. Thank heavens you're never too old ...

In other words, there is no need to worry about members of one's family and friends and acquaintances who think they 'know better' and who warn against a marriage on account of a marked difference in the ages of the persons concerned.

THE CHANGE OF LIFE –
IN MEN AS WELL AS WOMEN

A great deal has been said and written about the woman's change of life and the difficulties which can arise in connection with it. Formerly, many women believed that their sex lives were over. When menstruation ceased during their climacterium – as a rule between the ages of 45 and 50 – the chapter in their lives called 'sex' was over.

For many it was a relief. The women of former generations gave themselves up more 'for their country' than because they derived any pleasure from sexual intercourse. Unfortunately, they got nothing out of sexual relationships with their husbands and were only happy to have the excuse that 'now we're too old for that sort of thing'.

That they gave up was thus an expression of their resignation, their disappointment in sex, which had never given them anything but trouble. Many had furthermore during their change of life experienced mental and physical problems. It is our impression that the change of life today is not such a large problem for women as it was for their mothers and grandmothers. For one thing, women are more youthful today at the same age and for another, doctors are more skilful.

After their climacterium, women can have a few problems concerning dryness in the vagina and the fact that the walls of the vagina become thinner. Both these little deficiencies can usually be helped with hormone cream which can be obtained only with a prescription. Not just any old face cream which is advertised as being a hormone cream, but a special cream for this particular purpose which sometimes needs to be bought on prescription. In exceptional cases the woman may have to consult a gynaecologist.

For many years it was believed that the man didn't have any 'change of life'. Nor does he – physically – but mentally it may be said that he goes through one or two critical years.

Just because there are no outward physical signs, as in the case of the woman, which bear witness to some form of transition, we are inclined to ignore the symptoms in a man. In the man, his change of life is generally revealed in the form of fits of depression and a feeling of dissatisfaction.

These may in some cases be so violent that he has to go to hospital, or even cause him, in sheer desperation, to leave his wife, children and job.

It is as a rule at some time between the age of 40 and 50 that a man reviews his whole past life critically. 'How much have I achieved of all things I dreamed about when I was younger?' he asks himself.

'I'm going to be married to this person for the rest of my life. This furniture, this home, this street will all stare me in the face to the end of my days. I will have to keep the job I've got now until I'm pensioned off!' This is the sort of thing a man says to himself and looks round him disappointedly. 'This isn't what I dreamed about. Now I'm caught in a trap. Have I still got a chance of realizing the dreams of my youth?'

This sort of thing can represent a serious mental crisis for a man and how it ends may depend on several factors: his own strength, just how disappointed he is, how mature he is, etc., etc.

Very few people achieve all the things they dreamt of when they were young. It applies equally to both men and women that we – when we marry and bind ourselves to another person – more or less have to do some cold calculating: 'What am I going to do, and what am I going to gain by it?'

We cannot count on landing up in the position which would please us most. Marriage is not an ideal arrangement for two people, but today there is no better alternative. (Group sex and large communal families are the expression of a healthy experimental attempt to find something better, but it is by no means certain that either group sex or large communal families, in the forms in which they have been tried so far, will prove to be the solution.)

In all circumstances, what we must realize for the time being is that our objective must be to end up where we will find ourselves *least dissatisfied*.

This is not an expression of resignation but a realistic, positive philosophy of life.

DIFFICULTIES WITH THE PROSTATE

Men can also have physical problems when they get a little older. Quite a number have difficulty with the prostate and have to be operated on, and this can bring about various sexual difficulties, all of which can be overcome and which, as a rule, *are* also overcome. Men are very sensitive and concerned about their sexual organs, and the slightest difficulty, not to mention an operation, can give mental problems. But as a rule these are based on anxiety which is quite unfounded.

One problem which men may find themselves up against is that they can get an erection and have an orgasm all right but that no semen is ejaculated from the penis during orgasm. This may be precisely one of the after-effects of an operation on the prostate, and should not cause any worry at all. It makes absolutely no difference to the pleasure the man derives from intercourse. What happens is that the semen, instead of coming out of the penis, is pushed up into the bladder. If the man examines his urine the first time he passes water after an orgasm of this kind without producing any semen, he will find that his urine is very cloudy. This cloudiness has been caused by semen but there is nothing for him to worry about whatsoever. It is neither harmful nor wrong. As a rule he will also have been prepared for this eventuality by his doctor, but sometimes doctors don't always think of the fact that even elderly patients may have a sex life.

Another problem in older men can be heart attacks. Previously, doctors were inclined to dissuade patients with serious heart trouble from continuing their sex lives, but this was a somewhat unrealistic attitude.

The sex urge is there and demands – admittedly at greater intervals than in youth – to be satisfied. It is the same kind of problem that we find in pregnant women during the last part of their pregnancy. They too have reduced sexual urges but even these need satisfying.

There are three possibilities of obtaining satisfaction: nocturnal dreams, masturbation, and sexual activity with another person.

Nocturnal dreams and masturbation can certainly be just as taxing for both pregnant women and people with heart trouble as a pleasant and peacefully carried through session of sexual intercourse or other sexual togetherness. Which means to say that if you have heart trouble (or are pregnant) you should naturally take this fact into consideration and not embark on wild and exhausting acrobatics, but conduct your sexual activity in a more relaxed and peaceful way.

THERE IS ALWAYS MORE TO BE LEARNT

In the course of six chapters we have attempted to cover the most necessary and important things we feel you ought to know in order to achieve a happy sex life.

Attempted to ... ?

Yes, because there is much more within the sphere of modern sociology, more experience that has been gained from modern family and marriage counselling, details which we, despite all our efforts, have not had room to include, but which may happen to apply to your particular case. So all we can do is encourage you to continue your studies on your own. Several times in this book we have pointed out that there is plenty of literature to be had on sexual enlightenment and that one can always find something useful in most of these books. But there are one or two more recent works, which describe the observations made by modern researchers.

We would particularly recommend: *An Analysis of Human Sexual Response* by Ruth and Edward Brecher, likewise various books by Julius Fast, Julia and Jerome Rainer, Albert Ellis and Johan and June Robbins.

And then of course the great research work of modern sexology: Masters and Johnson, *Human Sexual Response* – for those who have the courage. It is extremely comprehensive and the most important parts of it are mentioned in the book by the Brechers listed above. Also in their latest book: *Sexual Inadequacy.*

We have devoted a lot of space to the technical side of sexual relationships and some of our readers will perhaps feel that we have neglected the spiritual and tender aspects. To a certain extent they are right. But we have our specific reasons.

First, it is precisely in the sphere of technique that research has got so much to tell us. Second, we feel it is our readers' problems which must determine what we write about most. It so happens we have never received a letter running as follows:

'We get on so wonderfully sexually, but we have never really understood what love is all about.'

On the other hand, we receive letters every day saying:

'We love each other dearly but I never get satisfied sexually, I never have an orgasm.'

Thus it would appear to be in the sphere of technique that most problems lie. Furthermore, it is very difficult to teach things like tact, consideration, understanding, finesse, maturity, etc., in a textbook.

If you will forgive us for reverting to the driving school

147

once more we would like to use another image and say: It's easy to teach people where the carburetter is, how to overtake or how to stop at the major road ahead sign. But nobody knows as yet quite how to change a smart aleck who is always taking chances into a considerate driver. That is more than the driving school can manage.

That is why driving instructors only mention things like consideration and carefulness in more general terms and instead concentrate on technical matters and the more obvious rules of the road. For without this knowledge one certainly would not be able to drive at all. Good driving technique at least reduces the risk of mistakes and accidents.

Good knowledge of sexual technique is just as useful. You should stand a greater chance of having a happy sex life with the knowledge you have now than without.

Finally, a word of advice. Pick up this book now and again and read it through in small portions. We have often heard from readers that they have only understood what we meant when they had read a section for the third or fourth time.

Perhaps at some time or other they have experienced something which suddenly shows up our claims in a new light. 'Oh, I *see*, that's what they meant!' Yes, maybe. Sexual relationships aren't very easy, either to understand or to describe. And you don't always find yourself in the seventh heaven. But then the sixth isn't so bad either.

Postscript

The attentive reader will perhaps have noticed that we have repeated ourselves several times in this book.

(Diligent readers of our writings will have come across the same lines of thought in our other books.)

We have several excuses. To start with, it often happens that we ourselves arc forced to hear new lines of thought several times before we can accept them. Second, this is not a book that can be read from cover to cover without putting it down. But many people will glance through it and read what happens to interest them or deal with their particular problem.

Finally, we would like to present two letters here. One of them is from a man and could have been written by many men. The other is from a woman. A great many women will recognize themselves.

A LETTER WHICH COULD HAVE BEEN WRITTEN BY EVERY MARRIED MAN

Dear Sten,

Presumably it is hopeless to ask. After all, you can't change people, but still.

Why does it always have to be in the dark, in bed, belly

to belly? 'Ow, ow, it hurts when you come in from behind!'

I think it's lovely!

The clitoris, the nerve centre of a woman's erotic feelings: 'No, not there – that's too hard, too gentle, too slow, too quick' – 'Try yourself, then!' – 'Do you think I'm going to do it to myself!'

After half an hour I've got a cramp in my arm. 'Oh, I was just about to come!'

In twenty years it has only once been a real success.

Am I really such a clumsy oaf?

Can women never feel spontaneous lust? To look at a man or to have urges?

Can women really go without for months on end?

Is there any connection between frigidity and the clitoris? In other words, that frigid women don't have one? Does size or position play any part? (Frank Harris says somewhere: As big as a thumb.)

A good job I'm *writing* to you so I don't need to hear you saying: 'Look here, Inge – this will make you laugh!'

Have women got special periods when they feel sexual urges, for example in conjunction with menstruation, ovulation, the seasons of the year, the weather or the like?

Men always have urges.

Tastes differ, I know, but for heaven's sake, is a stiff weapon really so hideous that a woman can't bear looking at it? Even a thirty-seven-year-old woman? The best she can manage is to hold it like a cigarette – once a year!

Otherwise, we have a wonderful family life, harmonious in every way – neither of us does any sidestepping, I can guarantee that. But perhaps I should let her have a try?

Because just imagine if somebody existed who could make her so wild that she'd start piddling in her bed.

Yes, I am quite undoubtedly more hot on her (*in love* sounds so damned silly after twenty years) than she is on me. She is luscious, appetizing and attractive.

After an evening during which lots of other men have watched her, turned round to look at her, smiled at her, etc. – am I perverse just because I prance around and can hardly wait till I'm alone with her before – well, you know where a fellow's hands make for, don't you?

'You never think of anything else.'

And later, in bed, little remarks like: 'I'm practically asleep.' Marital rights! Don't make me laugh! Once she has fallen asleep I take matters in my own hands.

Well, that was the sort of confession one doesn't often dare to make.

You know the trick of saying to a man: 'People who masturbate get hairs growing on the palms of their hands'? Nearly everybody immediately looks.

Drink? Yes, thanks, it helps a bit. But that would probably turn her into an alcoholic.

How often should people make love on an average?

Yours,

X

Dear X,

Thank you very much for a warm and sincere letter, which millions of men would have been able to write, even if they might not have been able to formulate it in such a lively fashion as you have done.

May we, however, despite this – in all friendliness – be a little hard on you?

We think you can stand it.

In asking your questions you jump from one line of thought to the next. May we answer in the same way?

'In the dark, in bed, belly to belly – why?'

We have said this so often: Women are slower to warm up sexually than men. It means that women, to an even greater degree than men, use their imagination, indulge in flights of fancy in order to arouse themselves the more. And if one is going to lie on one's back trying to imagine a very exciting sexual situation it is actually rather disturbing if the light is on in the room. Other factors also play a part. Our sex lives are still very secret, they still belong to the acts of darkness, and it gives a woman a certain feeling of security to be concealed by the dark.

Then there is the question of how you look at it. Note all the excellent books of sexual enlightenment which are being published nowadays. They are unrealistic from one point: everything is so beautiful, so sterile, so horribly 'designed by a professional architect'. It's like thumbing through the pictures in *Modern Homes* and then looking at one's own jumbled place. Nobody lives like that, nothing looks quite like that.

We aren't as beautiful, as well built – those of us who lie there trying to do the things the books write about. Nor are we so relaxed and cheerful as people in books are. We grimace, and we make sounds that are reminiscent of cows being drowned in a bog – and they come out at both ends too.

You must not expect your wife, who doesn't get anything out of her sex life, to find it exciting to get into the various, more or less acrobatic positions which men think are such fun, just because men manage to have orgasms quickly and easily. And from behind – well, it can be very nice for a man, but in that position we can guarantee that a woman doesn't stand much of a chance of getting anything out of it.

Later you write about 'Not there' and 'Not so hard'. What about trying an electric vibrator?

What is abundantly clear from your letter is that you make the same understandable mistake as the majority of other men, namely that of believing that women function in precisely the same way as men. (You have, however, begun to suspect that women can feel things in a different way.)

But how can men hope to know any better? Women themselves often pretend. Or else they are *all* desperately unhappy at the fact that they are not as sensual and lovely as other women. But the majority of women *do* respond more sluggishly than the majority of men.

Actually, you should be extremely happy that your wife is able to 'call the tune' at all. Who else, for heaven's sake, knows where, how hard or how fast she wants to be stimulated?

But you would appear to have just the right kind of temperament and the right, persevering spirit which is necessary to sort out a situation of this kind. Both you, and your wife in particular, deserve to have your joint efforts crowned with success.

It is important for your wife to understand that along with the equalizing process which the sexes are undergoing nowadays follows the right of the woman to procure her orgasm herself – though by all means together with the man. But it's not something he is supposed to make her a present of, and her own sexual satisfaction isn't supposed to be something which she makes *him* a present of either.

Her orgasm must not become a scalp in the belt of his vanity – it would then become an intolerable form of pressure on her. On the other hand, no matter how far the process of equalization of the sexes may have come, it is still the man who, lovingly, patiently, persistently and determinedly, must exercise a certain amount of pressure in order to get his wife going. Unfortunately, matters *are* this involved.

Spontaneous lust is not very common in women – their urges don't hover just below the surface, so to speak, as they do in most men. Women need a little more 'warming

153

up'. Women find it much easier than men to go for long periods without having their sexual urges satisfied.

If a woman is frigid, does it mean she hasn't got a clitoris? Aha, you gave yourself away there! You have read and learnt far too little from modern books on sexual enlightenment. Otherwise you would *know*, to start with, that *all* women have a clitoris (apart from those who live in those barbarian Arab and African countries where it is removed by an operation). Secondly, frigid women do not exist.

Frigid means *deep-frozen, cold, icy* – and no women are entirely devoid of the ability to have erotic feelings – and that includes your wife. But some women are more sensual than others. (We would like to mention that we didn't expose this gap in your knowledge in order to mock you, but rather to encourage you to study the subject in the many excellent books which are available nowadays.)

The size and position of the clitoris play absolutely no part in the degree of pleasure obtained by the woman – on the contrary.

Masters and Johnson have demonstrated that there are women with small clitorises who have more and better orgasms than women with large ones – and *vice versa*. Similarly, that a woman whose clitoris is situated far from the entrance to the vagina can have better orgasms than a woman whose clitoris lies immediately above the entrance – *and vice versa*. In other words, details like these are completely unimportant. (Frank Harris is a very entertaining writer, but a mendacious windbag when it comes to information about sexual matters. He also believed that a man could only have a specific number of ejaculations in the course of a lifetime and then that was that. In reality, of course, it is the other way round. The more ejaculations a man has the longer he is likely to maintain a vigorous sex life well into a ripe old age.)

No, we didn't laugh at all – on the contrary, we repeat that you have written a letter which covers an extraordinary number of the problems experienced by men.

154

A few women claim to have slightly more pronounced sexual feelings just before or just after a menstruation, or in the middle of the period (during the days when ovulation takes place). But pronounced periods of female sexual desire have not been discovered.

Masters and Johnson, however, relate that women during the middle three months of pregnancy often have better and more orgasms than they had before pregnancy. Also, that during the first and last three months they are, if anything, less interested in sex. Furthermore, Masters and Johnson relate that women who breast-feed their children would appear to recommence sexual activities with their husbands more quickly after giving birth than those who do not. The reason for this is possibly that the touching and sucking of the nipples releases a hormone which stimulates organs in the abdomen – for example, the womb. Some women can even have orgasms whilst suckling their children, a matter which unfortunately often gives rise to bad consciences – instead of relaxing and enjoying it as they ought to.

Basically speaking, men are always ready for sex, but their urges can naturally vary a little according to how hard they are working and other factors.

No, of course neither the female nor the male sexual organs are ugly in themselves – no uglier than a mouth or a nose. But then we have been brought up to believe that they should not be seen. In point of fact, a fully-grown young man who goes to bed with a girl for the first time has never before seen the female sexual organs at close hand – and a woman in the same situation has never seen an erected penis. And if the girl insists on darkness, neither of them have any chance of doing so in this case, either.

And so for both of them it can be something of a shock.

Another thing plays an even more important part. If you are hungry and have discovered that you can be satisfied by a steak – then you think that steak is about the loveliest thing you ever set eyes on.

If you are hungry and have a piece of chicken that tastes like cardboard pushed under your nose for the thousandth time, something which you have so many times before tried to sink your teeth into, but in vain – then you are likely to scream: 'Take that dreadful thing away!'

In other words, you must not expect your wife to think much of your sexual organ as long as she has not achieved any regular form of satisfaction from sexual relationships with you. And even then, one should bear in mind that it is not always the penis itself which gives her such satisfaction.

Thus her behaviour has very little to do with modesty. And we don't believe that anybody is *born* modest in this sense.

You think she is wonderful. We don't mind betting that she is touched by the fact that you – despite all your troubles – are still as 'hot' on her as you say you are.

And we feel that you should quite cynically exploit the fact that she *is* touched to tempt her to try a little experiment with you. There's nothing wrong about having a couple of drinks, for instance a bottle of strong beer or half a bottle of wine between the two of you, and it can sometimes be just enough to help a woman to relax her inhibitions a little.

You write in your very long letter that you force your wife to read our correspondence column, but now we're going to tell you something which we feel you should refrain from showing her if possible. It's a little trick. You're to tell your wife: 'I feel like going to bed with you every day!' if you really feel like doing so *every other day*.

Or, you should say: 'I feel like going to bed with you every other day,' if in reality you feel like doing so every three days. This will give her a feeling of being 'let off' once in a while, and it can be quite a nice feeling. In other words, you are to make demands upon her a little oftener than you really feel like doing. This will give her a feeling of having a say in the matter too.

It may sound very raw and cynical, as we have described it here – and it can easily be misunderstood. Please don't take it quite as literally as we have described it, but it does contain a psychological truth about *relativity*.

Perhaps we should put it in a different, slightly gentler way. If your wife tells you that she will only sleep with you once a month, but then actually does so once a week, you will be happy and grateful and think that she is sweet and willing.

If she promises to place herself at your disposal every day and then in point of fact only does so every other, you will feel annoyed and think you've been led up the garden path.

That is what we mean.

Incidentally, we believe that the majority of married couples between the ages of 30 and 60 or so sleep with each other approximately once or twice or three times a week.

And then: 'After half an hour I get cramp in my arm . . .' It is not uncommon for a woman to take between 15 and 45 minutes to reach her climax. And there is a difference between a man's sexual urges and a woman's, so don't let things get to the state where you *insist* on her having an orgasm every time.

Finally, may we remind you that it is precisely at your wife's age and yours that so many couples begin to get something out of their sex lives. Particularly the woman, that is.

THE LETTER A NUMBER
OF WOMEN MIGHT HAVE WRITTEN

Dear Inge and Sten Hegeler,

I am married for the second time and my husband is five years older than myself. We get on well together but it's not so good when we get on to the subject of sex. It is as if he simply cannot tolerate the idea that I know more

157

than he does. He says he has been to bed with several other women besides me. But that's not what I mean at all. I would just so like us to have as much pleasure from each other as possible.

I never get anything out of sleeping with my husband. His attitude is that we must both have an orgasm together at the same time.

What I want to ask is this. Is it actually possible at all? I know that many people believe it is, perhaps men in particular. If I tell him what I would like him to do, he thinks quite simply that I must be abnormal.

I would now like to ask you to tell him what is necessary in order for a woman to have an orgasm, and then I would like to show him your letter.

The whole difference between a woman and a man is that a woman can live her whole life and bear children – without ever having got any pleasure whatsoever out of sexual intercourse.

I presume that things are this way in so many marriages because the husband does not know what he is supposed to do – and perhaps the wife doesn't know it either. Maybe she derives some pleasure when her husband has his orgasm and thinks that this is the way she is supposed to get something out of it.

Perhaps the woman can become satisfied by love alone, or perhaps it doesn't matter so much to the woman as to the man whether she has an orgasm. I have thought of this possibility.

Am I completely wrong?

Yours sincerely,

(Mrs.) A. M.

Dear Mrs. A. M.

Thank you for your letter. We feel tempted to call it *The Letter From All Women*, but it wouldn't have been quite true, even though a tremendous number of women *could* have written it.

Your letter is so wise and so right that it almost makes one cry. Cry, because your husband does not seem to realize how extremely wise and normal a wife he has.

We think you are so completely right. Shall we start by confirming that *he is* the person in the world who knows the most about *himself* – and that *you* are the person in the world who knows most about *you*.

So when your husband says that he also has had experience with other girls, perhaps this experience doesn't apply to you. To this must be added the fact that so very many women lie in order to make a man feel wonderful. And in many ways this is a risky thing to do.

The dream that both partners *must* have simultaneous orgasms is quite simply a myth. Naturally it is wonderful and fantastic if you and your partner manage to achieve it together every once in a while – but it is a very rare thing which only the most skilful and those who have most confidence in each other can manage occasionally.

It *can* be done then, but it requires years of experimentation; also, that both partners are so certain of their own and the other person's orgasm that they can control things according to the other's progress.

Unfortunately your husband seems to suffer from the usual, old-fashioned kind of masculine pride and vanity to the extent that he does not want to learn anything and does not wish to be directed. No doubt he will dismiss the whole matter as 'rubbish' and maintain that one can easily manage one's sex life without all these little tricks – and that you are abnormal.

But he's wrong. And it's a pity for both of you if he refuses to listen. The normal thing is that it is much more difficult for a woman to achieve an orgasm than it is for by far the majority of men.

Only very few women are able to have an orgasm almost just as easily through ordinary sexual intercourse as the normal man.

During ordinary sexual intercourse with the penis inside the vagina, the smaller vaginal lips are gently tugged at, and these smaller vaginal lips are connected to the prepuce (or foreskin) on the clitoris – which is just like a tiny little penis. In this way the nerves on the clitoris are stimulated and in very rare cases this can be sufficient.

In all too many marriages the woman has given up and believes that she is frigid (but frigid women don't exist). And of course you are not a frigid woman, you just want to keep on trying until you manage to get something out of your sexual relationship with your husband, which is why we won't call your letter *The Letter From All Women.*

Your husband should be grateful and kiss you – on lots of your most sensitive places.

Let us hear from you again! Let us know when the sun begins to appear over the edge of the horizon – or whether the darkness continues to lie heavily over your part of the country!

A sex life is something we have for many years. Ideally, it should get better and better, but never perfect